The Power of
I AM

Volume 3

Compiled, Edited, Formatted & Layout

By

Shanon Allen

&

David Allen

Books for Enlightening and Illuminating the Mind

Copyright © 2017 by Shanon Allen / David Allen

All rights reserved. No part of this publication may be reproduced, distributed, or transmitted in any form or by any means, including photocopying, recording, or other electronic or mechanical methods, without the prior written permission of the publisher, except in the case of brief quotations embodied in critical reviews and certain other noncommercial uses permitted by copyright law. Printed in the United States of America

First Paperback Edition, January 2017

ISBN: 978-0-9972801-7-3

Visit Us At **NevilleGoddardBooks.com** for a complete listing of all our books and **1000's of Free Books to Read online and download.**

Published
by
Shanon Allen

Copyright © 2017

Preface

Due to the overwhelming response to The Power of I AM, 1 and 2, I have decided to add to the series, Volume 3. It is with my utmost sincerity and appreciation, not only of my personal discovery of I AM, but that circumstances have allowed me to be a part of a process which makes it available to many throughout the world. The comments that are left for my books do not go unappreciated and are a large part of my motivation to brining more quality books to the world of metaphysics and the law of attraction.

Thank you everyone.

Foreword

I have taken the liberty to use as the foreword to "The Power of I AM, Volume 3", from part of "An After Word" from William Walker Atkinson's, The Secret of Success, as it seems fitting to this, the third installment of The Power of I AM Series by David Allen.

In this little work we have endeavored to call your attention to something of far greater importance than a mere code of rules and general advice. We have pointed out to you the glorious fact that within each of you there is a Something Within, which if once aroused would give you a greatly increased power and capacity. And so we have tried to tell you this story of the Something Within, from different viewpoints, so that you might catch the idea in several ways.

We firmly believe that Success depends most materially upon a recognition and manifestation of this Something Within . . we think that a study of the character and work of all successful men will show you that differ as they do in personal characteristics, they all manifest that consciousness of that Something Within them that gives them an assurance of Inward Power and Strength, from which proceeds Courage and Self-Confidence. You will find that the majority of successful men feel that there is a Something helping them . . back of and behind their efforts. Some have called this Thing by the name of "Luck" or "Destiny," or some such term. But it is all a form of the same recognition of an Inward Power that they are "helped" in some way, although they are not quite sure of the nature of the helper . . in fact, the majority of them do not stop to speculate upon its nature, they are too busy and are content with the knowledge that It is there.

This Something Within is the Individual . . the "I" in each of them . . the source of the power which men manifest when they express it. And this little book is written in the hopes that to many it may be the first step toward the recognition, unfoldment and manifestation of this Inward Power. We earnestly urge upon you to cultivate this "I AM" consciousness . . that you may realize the Power Within you.

And then there will come naturally to you the correlated consciousness which expresses itself in the statement, "I CAN and I WILL," one of the grandest affirmations of Power that man can make. This "I Can and I Will" consciousness is that expression of the Something Within, which we trust that you will realize and manifest. We feel that behind all the advice that we can give you, this one thing is the PRIME FACTOR in the Secret of Success.

William Walker Atkinson - The Secret of Success

Acknowledgments

I would like to extend a deep appreciation to the following authors, all of which have left the world with a priceless knowledge of this great power that exists in all men. As with all my books, most of which have been compiled and edited from books in the public domain, I take extreme measures to insure that I do not violate any copyrights. I also feel that my compilations offer a unique approach since many of editing's have taken the best parts of those books and complied them into one book.

Benjamin Johnson, Charles Fillmore, Charles Haanel, Christian Larson, Edna Lister, Emmet Fox, Ernest Holmes, Eugene Del Mar, Fenwicke L. Holmes, Florence Gloria Crawford. Frances Larimer Warner, Franklin Fillmore Farrington, H. Emilie Cady, Helen Wilmans, Henry Harrison Brown, Jane Woodard, Joseph Murphy, Nancy McKay Gordon, Neville Goddard, Orison Swett Marden, Robert A. Russell, Walter C Lanyon, William Walker Atkinson / Yogi Ramacharaka

CONTENTS

260 I AM Quotes					9

"The Power of The I AM" by Walter Devoe		181

"The I AM is the Way" by Christian Larson		185

"What AM I? by Orison Swett Marden		198

5 Blank Pages for Notes				214

Books by David Allen				219

The Power Within, The Great "I AM

The beginning of each quote is in **bold** print.

There is no one thing which will give a timid soul such assurance, which will so brace up one who is inclined to depreciate and efface himself, as the constant affirmation of the " I AM." " I AM courage; I AM health, vigor, strength; I AM power; I AM peace; I AM plenty; I AM a part of abundance, because I AM one with the very Source of Infinite Supply. I AM rich, because I AM heir to all the resources of the universe."

Stoutly, constantly, everlastingly affirm that you will become what your ambitions indicate as fitting and possible. Do not say " I shall be a success sometime"; say, " I AM a success. Success is my birthright." Do not say that you are going to be happy in the future. Say to yourself, " I was intended for happiness, made for it, and I AM happy."

God, the Father of all life is in you! Being all imagination, your true name is I AM, and besides you there is no other God. So I tell you: unless you believe "I AM He," you will die in your sins in the sense that you will continue missing the mark. You must assume that you are now the man (the woman) you want to be and persist in that assumption, for there is no other way for you to be it, as there is only God (imagination) in this world.

SPIRIT KNOWS ITSELF

God (I AM) speaks and it is done; but if God speaks, His Word must be Law. The Word of God is also the Law of God. God is Word, God is Law and God is Spirit; this is self-evident. We arrive at the conclusion that God, as Spirit, is Self-Conscious Life. That Spirit is conscious is proven by the fact that we have evidence of this consciousness strewn through all time and space. God must know that God Is. This is the inner meaning of the teaching of the "I AM," handed down from antiquity. "The Spirit is the Power that knows Itself," is one of the oldest sayings of time.

Since I AM as I think I AM, I have heretofore lived the slave of conditions and subject of environment because God and I were two. But now, no longer separated, the prodigal has arisen and come home to the Father and in Unity found Power, and in this realization has conquered disease and death, and, chanting "I and my Father are one," he has taken heaven by violence and, planting its Love and Truth upon earth, made all the promised heaven here and now.

Matter and body cannot create, because they are effects.
They can only manifest the energy infused into them by their cause. Vitality is not a material force; it is spiritual force. Vitality is cause. Vitality is the creative energy of the love and intelligence of the I AM which holds in its embrace every atom of sentient substance. It is the vitality of the Infinite Mind that we see manifesting in bird and beast, tree and flower, and this same vitality is at this moment giving you all the life that you have, and the Infinite Mind can give you as much as you can individualize and express. Your lack of knowledge of the possibilities of your own nature keeps you from growing out of your weak or sickly condition. Knowledge is power.

Man knows intuitively that he is God's supreme creation
and that dominion and power are his, though he does not understand fully. The I AM of him ever recognizes the one divine source from which he sprang, and he turns to it endeavoring to fathom its wonderful secrets.

It is done unto you as you believe. We limit the expression of the I AM through our belief in limitation. The Divine Law will produce anything we choose. It will produce prosperity instead of poverty, health instead of sickness. The Law is, but It must be definitely specialized. Until we specialize It, It is only a latent possibility. Through this Law, we set the Principle in which we live in motion. When we do not use the Law consciously and constructively, we are using It unconsciously and, it may be, destructively. Prayer is the mental act through which we specialize the Law for specific purposes. In the Silence, we are responsive to the Law. Silence is the home of the soul. It is always at rest, always at peace, always in repose. The unseen and silent forces in the universe are the strongest. Physical activity is noisy and slow; Infinite activity is silent and quick. We hear nothing as gravity holds our material world together. There is no sound as the sun each day lifts billions of tons of water from the earth. Neither is there any perceptible friction or noise in the operation of electricity. What we interpret as such is disturbance in the manifestation and not in the power itself.

The I AM is indifferent to things because it recognizes nothing apart from Itself. It desires only man's unity with Itself. In this unity man embodies his Good. In the intangible world of Spirit, all things needful to man are classified under the heading of Good. If we seek the supremacy of Good (God), we shall never lack. Not until we withdraw our thought from the relative plane are we able to cultivate our inner resources.

Inasmuch as this great Mind is flowing into our bodies, it must of necessity have an outlet. This conclusion leads us to accept the following: The Universal Mind flows through us, but registers or localizes itself in the solar plexus and from this point radiates by thought to the world. Therefore we see that God (I AM) is the only Thinker, Actor, Power and Life. Then "I AM" Success or if it would be easier for the student to realize the impersonal, he may say, "I AM is Success." If he wishes to say, "God is Success," he is saying the same thing.

It is not so much what we say, so far as the words are concerned; it is the understanding with which we say them.

Troward says, "I AM that which I contemplate." You become what you claim and feel yourself to be. Except you now believe and accept as true that you now are what you long to be, you will remain as you are. In other words, you will die in your sins, meaning you will fail to reach your mark in life. If a man who is poverty stricken refuses to enter into the mood of opulence and the belief in a God of abundance forever supplying all his needs, he will remain poor regardless of the church he joins or what creed he adopts.

The Law

I AM hard as adamant, cold as steel, bitter as gall, deadly as poison; I AM soft as down, warm as sunlight, gentle as a zephyr, tender as a mother. I AM your adversary, your opponent, your enemy; I AM your counselor, your assistant, your friend. I AM stronger than the strongest, I bend you to my iron will; I AM yielding to the uttermost, gladly I go your way. I AM a curse; I AM a blessing. I AM what you make of me; I thwart or serve, I degrade or exalt; I AM your Master or your servant. Obey me, and you are my Master ; Disobey, and you are my slave. I AM the Law!

In the 12th chapter of the Book of Numbers, we are told: "If there is a prophet among you, I the Lord will make myself known unto him in a vision and I will speak with him in a dream." A scriptural prophet is not one who tells your fortune, but one who hears the Word of God and fulfills it. If you asked me if I were a prophet I would answer in the affirmative. I am not one who prophesies by looking into a crystal ball, teacup leaves, cards, or astrology, but one who has fulfilled scripture. I know I AM the central figure of scripture called "the Father." I came into the world to fulfill scripture and share my revelations, my experiences concerning the power to create. In this simple way God revealed his power to create, his power to remember when!

When the average person employs the term "ego," he thinks that he is dealing with something that is hidden so deeply in the abstract that it can make but little difference whether we understand it or not. This, however, does not happen to be true, because it is the ego that must act before any action can take place anywhere in the human system, and it is the ego that must originate the new before any step in advance can be taken. And in addition, it is extremely important to realize that the power of will to control the forces we possess, depends directly upon how fully conscious we are of the ego as the ruling principle within us. We understand therefore, that it is absolutely necessary to associate all thought, all, feeling and all actions of mind or personality with the ego, or what we shall hereafter speak of as the " I AM." The first step to be taken in this connection, is to recognize the "I AM" in everything you do, and to think always of the "I AM," as being you, the supreme you. Whenever you think, realize that it is the "I AM" that originated the thought. Whenever you act, realize that it is the " I AM" that gives initiative to that action, and whenever you think of yourself or try to be conscious of yourself, realize that the "I AM" occupies the throne of your entire field of consciousness.

If the world of "things" still has any hold on you and you have not realized that you are Mind out of which all "things" flow, then you may have to let "things" go. But once you do and you realize that I AM Mind, and you begin to "praise God/Mind . . from Which all blessings flow," you will no longer be held in bondage to things, no longer feel you need to hold onto, keep, save, or hoard "things," for you will know creation, or "things" are Spirit, presently manifested in the moment, continually. I manifest, or make visible the world, body, forms, things that I see, hear, touch, smell, taste, etc. as my "world" of awareness. But they are in me! They are all IN MIND! They are Me, The Mind I AM, not separate from,

but in and of Me. Spirit . . All is Spirit. They have no substance in and of themselves. They are proceeding in the moment from God-Consciousness. Someone with a poverty consciousness brings forth lack, but it is an illusion, although it seems "real" to them. Someone with a religious consciousness brings forth the law of their particular belief system, and although it is an illusion, it sure seems "real" and necessary at the "time." Someone with a consciousness of illness and disease reflects illness and disease in a body they think they live in, but again, that is merely an illusion, for here now is the Perfect body I AM, and It is All.

In the degree that you perceive, recognize, and realize your essential identity with ME (I AM), the Supreme Presence-Power, the Ultimate Reality, in that degree will you be able to manifest My Spiritual Power. I AM over and above you, under and beneath you, I surround you on all sides. I AM also within you, and you are in ME; from Me you proceed and in Me you live and move and have your being. Seek Me by looking within your own being, and likewise by looking for Me in Infinity, for I abide both within and without your being. If, and when, you will adopt and live according to this Truth, then will you be able to manifest that Truth . . in and by it alone are Freedom and Invincibility, and true and real Presence and Power, to be found, perceived, realized and manifested.

If Christ is your own wonderful human imagination and all things . . be they good, bad, or indifferent . . are made by him, you can imagine unlovely things and perpetuate their image. To say that Christ makes only the good and a devil makes the evil is false. When you doubt the power of Christ in you . . that's the devil. Unless you actually believe that "I AM" is the being you are seeking and pray only to him by exercising your human imagination, you will never reach your desire, for awareness is the only power that can give it to you, imagination.

Not infrequently, patients who are students in Christian Science have had enough treatment to heal them a hundred times, but it is very difficult to get them to say, "I AM healed," even when there is every evidence to show they are healed, and there is nothing the matter but a little bit of fear, or a large measure, as the case may be. But it is difficult to get them to take their stand and say, "I AM healed." And yet in hundreds of cases, if people could say, "I AM healed," and stick to it, they would have the evidence very shortly. The mesmeric tendency of human beliefs, self pity, self condemnation, or self-something else, hinders that most important and scientific declaration.

A study of the psychological nature of man verifies the belief in "The Trinity" running through all Life. Man is self-conscious; of this we are sure, for he can say "I AM." This fact alone proves his claim to immortality and greatness. In psychology we learn that man is threefold in his nature; that is, he has a self-conscious mind, a subconscious mind and a body. In metaphysics we learn that the three are but different attributes of the same life. Man's self-conscious mind is the power with which he knows; it is, therefore, one with the Spirit of God; it is, indeed, His only guarantee of conscious being.

As Jesus said, if you try to climb up some other way, you are a thief and a robber, and only trouble will come that way. He is emphasizing again the need for strict control of one's thoughts if one is to achieve that which he really desires. Jesus follows up this idea by saying, "I AM the door of the sheep; by me if any man enter in he shall be saved." The Jesus Christ teaching is the gateway to salvation, not in some distant heaven but in the immediate now. The "door" or "gate" is another very important Bible symbol. Passing through a door or a gate signifies a change in consciousness. When you pass from one room to another, or from one field to another, symbolically you pass from one state of mind to another. "Gate" or "door" means understanding and it also signifies dominion or power. In the Bible we so often find two different meanings or two aspects of the same thing. In this case the two meanings are supplementary . . understanding and dominion. Understanding gives dominion, and understanding comes with a change in consciousness.

You need to withdraw from the vexations of the world two or three times a day to center your thoughts in the quiet place of your own I AM. As you affirm the sacred name of the Divine Being (I AM), you will find rest from your disturbing worries, and in this interior state of peace, you will see more clearly how to will and to plan for a more successful experience.

When you know what you want, use your sense of feeling.
Let the feeling of satisfaction so fill your being that the idea ceases to be a desire, but has evoked motor elements. These awaken sensory sensations within you causing the desire's fulfillment. Imagination is nothing more than sensory states. Learn to go beyond an idea by feeling its reality. Then turn to another and still another, as the being who is feeling it begins to awaken within you. Fulfill all of your desires while you are here, and then when you least expect it, the Divine Breath will breathe upon that immortal tomb where you are buried. And you will awaken to find yourself completely sealed in your Holy Sepulcher where you have been dreaming your life into being. This world is made up of horrible dreams which the one within every individual is dreaming. That one must and will awaken, as you hear the story and put it into practice through repentance. The word "repentance" comes from the Greek word "metanoia," which means "a radical change of attitude." This change must be so radical that it gets right down to the root, the I AM! Think of your world as your mirror. Do you like what you see there? You know you can live with it or ignore it, but perhaps you would like to see it differently. If you would, repent by persuading yourself that you are seeing a world to your liking. Persist in your repentance, for to the degree that you are self-persuaded it is so, it will be so.

Repeat: . . "**Infinite Substance within me,** Infinite Supply flowing through me and to me, Infinite Activity around me and within me, Infinite Intelligence within me, directing me, guarding me, governing me, controlling me; the One and Only within me and through me, that is, Almighty God within me. There is no other, or beside which there is none other. Infinite love within me, seeing all, knowing all, loving all, One in and through all." Carry this concept out until you see that you live in everybody and everybody lives in you.

Then continue: "Infinite One, comprehending, seeing, knowing, understanding, living in and including the All, within me." Realize what this means. "I AM One with all people. There are no enemies. There is only the One, in all and through all."

While you are educating your intellect in the principles of truth, keep your heart very close to the loving consciousness of the Ever-Present. Let the immanent All Power in you be fed and strengthened daily and hourly by communion and cooperation with the transcendent I AM within, that you may embody the Power of this enlightening Presence for all humanity. Let your mortal spirit be bathed in the healing stream of Divine Thought, that you may become transformed into the health and perfection of an immortal soul of the Ever-Present's inspiration.

Throughout the Bible the writers speak of the Name of God or the Name of the Lord. For instance, when the Queen of Sheba, whom Jesus called the Queen of the South, came to visit Solomon, the Bible says that she came to test him with hard questions. She came to inquire, not about God, or about the Lord, but about the NAME of the Lord . . thus again emphasizing the Name. The key to the name of the Lord is found in what we call Jehovah, the personalized God of the Old Testament. Here we begin to get a sense of God expressing Himself as Man. Pure, unconditioned Being . . I AM THAT I AM . . has now become differentiated as men and women. The word Jehovah is an anglicized version of the Hebrew, which was made up of four letters, Yod, He, Wau, Hé . . spelling "Yevé." These four Hebrew letters represent the masculine and feminine principles, and in this form they mean one God (I AM) expressing Himself in the souls of men and women. The Hebrews went further with this idea of God and added suffixes, Jehovah becoming Jehovah-Ramah, Jehovah-Jire, and so on . . God as peace, God as health, God as abundance, etc.

The "breath of life" is a super-conscious reality. It is the essence of the "I AM." It is pure "Being" or Universal Substance, and our conscious unity with it enables us to localize it, and thus exercise the powers of this creative energy.

In the King James Bible the Hebrew "Jehovah" has been translated "Lord." Lord means an external ruler. Bible students say that Jehovah means the self-existent One, the I AM. Then instead of reading "Lord" we should read I AM. It makes a great difference whether we think of I AM, self-existence within, or "Lord," master without. All Scripture shows that Jehovah means just what God told Moses it meant: I AM. "This is my name for ever, and this is my memorial unto all generations." So instead of "Lord" say I AM whenever you read it and you will get a clearer understanding and realization of what Jehovah is.

Take my message to heart. The God spoken of in scripture is seated right here. He is in everyone as their wonderful human imagination. When you say, "I AM," that's God. If, right now you are assuming that you are other than what reason says you are and I ask you, "Who is imagining?" you would say, "I AM." At that very moment you have spoken God's name and all things are possible to God. So without the consent of anyone you can move from where you are to where you would like to be by a simple change of attitude. But your move must be fixed so that when you wake or sleep you remain in that attitude, for the state to which your thoughts constantly return constitutes your dwelling place, and your world is forever externalizing your dwelling place.

The Creator will give you generously of the Infinite Life and Power that springs from an Ever-Present Source. The Eternal Power in you can give you a more vigorous heart. Your digestive system can be re-energized. You can make a demand upon the Creator's power within you for a rich and healthy constitution, and that demand will be recognized and fulfilled. The same Power that created your tissues, glands and organs is still present within you and is always ready to recreate them when the appropriate conditions of mind and body are applied. That same Intelligent Power, which formed your organism from the original cells and then diversified them to create your liver, kidneys, muscles, bones and brain, this instant is willing to do as much and more than It has done for you in the past if you will only allow your lesser self to step aside so that that Power can be expressed. It is already expressing through you every moment. Think what a miracle it is that the intelligence of the Creator is this instant creating the right kind of metabolic constituents that you need through the action of millions of cells in your body. When you turn your attention to this matter of your own life, you will behold so great a wonder that, you will want no other or greater proof of the existence of an intelligent Creator. The wonder and mystery of your being will awaken a great awe within you. You will realize that you are "fearfully and wonderfully made." This awe is the awakening of your faculties of spiritual awareness which can know and feel the presence of the I AM. This awe of the Creator is the beginning of wisdom.

Jesus, who has clearly revealed the Father in His consciousness, tells all men how it came about. He points out the way. He says, "I AM the way, and the truth, and the life"; but there is always a condition attached to its realization by the seeker. He must "believe," he must "keep my words," "follow me." Summed up, the condition is that by adopting Jesus' methods you will find the same place in the Father that He found. But the Father is Spirit and spiritual understanding is the open sesame to His kingdom. The secrets of Jesus' words may be said to be in sealed packages to be opened by those only to whom is given "the mystery of the kingdom of God."

Ask yourself: "If I now believe that I AM He that the world worships as the Lord, and all things are possible to me, then I must test myself and according to my faith in myself will it be done unto me." It is up to the individual to perform the action, for the evidence always follows the action. Act as though things are as you would like them to be. Persuade yourself that it is true and let the results follow. This is how you are called upon to operate in this world. This is imagination. It is not written in detail, but only sketches that you fill in with your life.

"I AM here, I AM there, I AM everywhere." I AM within all, within every fiber, nerve, and cell of your being. I AM in the inanimate as well as the animate . . I AM everywhere. I AM everything and everywhere; call upon ME and see if I will not open the windows of Divine substance. I AM THAT I AM . . that particular I AM Consciousness which should come to this condition or situation to make its nothingness appear . . to cause it to release the power that lies hidden there, and which has caused you to fear. I AM ALL IN ALL . . I AM everywhere. No matter wither you go, into what locality, I AM there . . I have gone before you, because I AM already there and always have been there. I have already caused myself to be so impressed upon you that you find everything already prepared before you arrive. You find everything answered before you ask. You find everything supplied before you need. It is well with you . . do you hear? . . irrespective of person, place, or thing. It is well with you, irrespective of teachings of any nature whatsoever. I AM . . I AM . . I AM.

I AM as Conscious Law, that which I think, I AM, and since Thought is creative, I live in the world I think into existence. The real world of imagination, the subconscious world of Mind.

As you assert your I AM and become more and more positive with faith in the strength of your own personality, acquaintances may think you are becoming egotistical. but you are becoming one with the Creator! Because the world has not seen the truth that humanity is one with the Creator, it has failed to personify the Ever-Present and to build a paradise of health and prosperity on earth. You will arouse needless opposition to your desires and plans, if you tell what you think and plan to people who need not know.

Do not waste your faith and force contending against unnecessary opposition by revealing all the creative activities of your mind to doubters. Generate the force of your desire in secret until your intense spiritual influence compels all minds and conditions to respond to your goodwill and bring your desire to fruition. Whether you intensify your will to become an inspired artist, an organizer of production from the soil, the creator of an ideal home, or a teacher of children, remember to keep the thought of "service above self" uppermost. Become a lover and server of humanity, working always for the welfare of the whole, and your personality will become inspired by the more positive Power in the universe, the love of the Divine Will for all that lives. As you practice with us, you will grow to sense the personal power we have gained, and you will want to walk with us in the Way of the Creator. As your I AM and our I AM vibrate in unison, and through our attunement with the Infinite I AM, you will see and sense the Divine Wisdom.

If we start any such demonstration and try to apply the I AM to personality, we fall short. This is frequently the cause of lack of results in carrying out the laws that all metaphysicians recognize as fundamentally true. The mind does not always comprehend the I AM in its highest, neither does it discern that the all-knowing, omnipotent One is within man. This recognition must be cultivated, and everyone should become conscious of the I AM presence. This consciousness will come through prayer and meditation upon Truth. In Truth there is but one I AM, Jehovah, the omnipotent I AM that is eternally whole and perfect. If you take Jehovah-shalom into your mind and hold it with the thought of a mighty peace, you will feel a consciousness, a harmonizing stillness, that no man can understand. This consciousness is healing in itself. It must be felt, realized, and acknowledged by your individual I AM before the supreme I AM can pour out its power. Then you will know that you have touched something; but you cannot explain to another just what it is, because you have gone beyond the realm of words and made union with the divine cause. It is the quickening of your divinity through the power of the word. This divine nature is in us all, waiting to be brought into expression through our recognition of the power and might of the I AM.

Spiritual energy comes from within. The I AM is the source of Divine Energy. It flows through the consciousness of man as an impersonal, silent and Omnipresent Power. Through his soul (subjective mind), man makes his conscious approach to the Universal Mind. To be conscious of It is to be in vital touch with It, to give It conscious direction in body and affairs. Mind meets us at the level of our own understanding and manifests according to our consciousness. Since It cannot give us more than we can receive, we must be consciously receptive to It. Our work in the Silence is dynamic, the results differing according to our various states of consciousness.

GIVE US THIS DAY OUR DAILY BREAD The bread spoken of here refers not alone to food, clothing and money, but to the Bread of Life. Man shall not live by bread alone, but by every word that proceedeth out of the mouth of God. The law of increase is in the word. I AM is the active agent of creation. It externalizes itself in the substance that coexists with it. I AM the bread of life. Give us this day our daily bread. These words literally mean to you, "I AM positive to the Substance of the I AM here and now. I am receptive to It. My needs are met." The word 'give' is a command to Substance. You are not begging, pleading or beseeching. You are affirming the Truth, identifying yourself with It and accepting It.

Persist in your imaginal acts and the world will respond. The world does not cause, it only responds to your imaginal acts, for only God (I AM) acts and God (I AM) is in you as your own wonderful human imagination. Now, before you judge it, try it. If you do, you cannot fail, and when you prove imagination in the testing, share the good news with your brothers. Tell everyone you meet how the world works. You do not have to have a proper educational or social background to apply this principle; and you cannot fail, for an assumption, though false, if persisted in will harden into fact.

Any attempt to move anything out of the body or the circumstances, anything which does not have a cause in Divine Mind, will nullify the demonstration. Disagreeable conditions have no existence whatever outside of consciousness; therefore we must look to our own thoughts for a solution of our problems. The human body and the body of one's affairs will automatically express the prevailing state of thought in the mind. When we discover that our Mind is the Mind of God, that His Power is our Power, we shall be so close to Him that He will be in everything we do. When the I AM is given dominion over our consciousness, it works perfectly. Realizing this, we can walk perfectly, hear perfectly and see perfectly. Let this mind be in you.

When men evolve spiritually to a certain degree, they open up inner faculties that connect them with cosmic Mind, and attain results that are sometimes so startling that they seem to be miracle workers. What seems miraculous is the action of forces on planes of consciousness not previously understood. When a man releases the powers of his soul, he does marvels in the sight of the material-minded, but he has not departed from the law. He is merely functioning in a consciousness that has been sporadically manifested by great men in all ages. Man is greater than all the other creations of God-Mind because he has the ability to perceive and to lay hold of the ideas inherent in God-Mind and through faith bring them into manifestation. Thus evolution proceeds by man's laying hold of primal spiritual ideas and expressing them in and through his consciousness. In the exercise of his I AM identity man needs to develop certain stabilizing ideas. One of them is continuity or loyalty to Truth. In the Scriptures and in life we have many examples of how love sticks to the thing on which it has set its mind. Nothing so tends to stabilize and unify all the other faculties of mind as love. That is why Jesus gave as the greatest commandment that we love God.

Everything said in scripture is all about you, for you are the being called God, but unless you claim it you cannot attain it. How can you when you are the only power? You must walk conscious of being imagination, or die in your sins and never attain that awareness. No physical man made the statement: "Unless you believe that I AM He you will die in your sins." The one speaking is He who said these words: "I AM from above. You are from below. You are of this world, I AM not of this world." When Jesus Christ was publicly portrayed as crucified (remember, this play did not take place on earth save as a parable), he came before Pilate, who said: "Do you not know that I have the power to set you free or the power to crucify you?" And Jesus answered: "You have no power unless it has been given you from above."

Your I AMness is from above. Having come to do the Father's will, I who am now aware of being you, will drink the cup of experience to the very end. But no one has any power over me save I, by my assumption, give it away. I do it by assuming I am less than another, thereby forcing him to play the part of one superior to me. Everyone reflects my assumptions and plays their part relative to that which I have assumed, for there is nothing but Imagination, and I AM He. Assuming I am afraid, I live in a world of fear, for there is no other. Being protean, I am playing every part in my dream of life, be it for my good or for my ill.

I AM a Thought, an Idea of God, and that Idea is perfect even as my Father is perfect. I AM subjectively perfect, and that perfection is unfolding itself into objective expression.

All eternity will be required for the expression of that perfection which I AM. I AM an immortal child of God, and am NOW living the one only life of man, that of Self Consciousness, and I am coming each day more into the realization of myself as Love and Law. Life from itself has built in me an organism, and has thus become aware of its Self-creative power. If I can materialize flesh, the highest possible vibration in so-called matter, I can create any of the lesser forms. I AM the ultimate of Evolution, for my body allows perfect expression of my thought. As a Human Soul, through incarnation I AM expressing daily my perception of God, and as he creates in the subconscious my body and its environment, I am learning, by seeing Him work, how to become myself the creator of environment at will.

What the I AM has become through ages of experience, we are potentially. The Ever-Present comes with hosts of emancipated souls to help us conquer the limitations of our mortal natures, the limitations humanity has created, and to enthrone the divinity of the Infinite in all humanity.

Events and experiences are living things too, and they also seek and follow after their food. The food of events is thought. Your habitual thoughts nourish your conditions and cause them to increase and multiply. Fear thoughts, gloomy and critical thoughts, selfish thoughts, are the food of unhappiness, sickness, and failure. When you supply this food in abundance these things come into your life . . because they seek their food. Thoughts of God, thoughts of kindness, of optimism, and good will, are the food of health, joy, and success; and if you furnish a bountiful supply of this food you will attract these things instead. When you want to get some condition out of your life, starve it out by refusing to furnish any of the food upon which it thrives, and you will be surprised how rapidly it will leave you. It will go away in a hurry somewhere else, where its food is obtainable. "I AM the bread of life."

The great I AM is not far away from man. Spirit is closely connected with the little things of daily life. "The Kingdom of God is come nigh unto you." This means that the mighty One is with us in all ways. We are all in touch, heart with heart, and a real sympathy makes us one. In reality we all love the simple life. The pomp and parade and pageantry of the external world do not satisfy the soul. It is the small things that touch the heart and appeal to us.

In Mental Science, the great principle laid down is this:
Man is conjoined to the Eternal Life Principle. He is that Principle . . its very self in objectivity . . and in proportion as he becomes intellectually conscious of this tremendous truth, he finds an unfailing supply to all his needs, and grows more into a knowledge of his own mastery. We are manifestations of the unchanging Life Principle; of the Universal Spirit of Being; the inextinguishable I AM. It is the soul to nature . . the body. It is internal man. Man is the external of it. And the seeming two are one. This Law, or Principle, is man in subjectivity. Visible man is the Law, or Principle, in objectivity.

In the Silence, we manifest in our consciousness the Spirit of God. Through our positive and constructive thinking, the individual mind becomes one with the Absolute Universal Mind, making perfect realization possible. As we turn away from the world of the senses, we enter the Within, the Source of all things. God is unity; man is diversity. United, they manifest harmony, the true expression of the Silence. The soul is the constant expression of the I AM. It is the same whether Universal or individual. Heaven and harmony mean the same thing; when we work and think in harmony, all our action is constructive.

Begin now to hear the soft tread of the unseen guest of your heart, your desire. Open your mind and heart and let in your heart's desire. Welcome it! Say, "This is from God (I AM), a message of inspiration, and new life." This is God (I AM) letting you accept your good enthusiastically and lovingly. The embodiment of your inner urges will take place in response to such faith and devotion on your part.

Do not be concerned with the horrors of the world; simply remember that all is ordered and correct. Instead, fall in love with the I AM within you and change your world. God made it as it is now and he can change it, for your husband is a creator. Everything in your world can be traced back to your own wonderful human imagination, who is God (I AM). Fall in love with the state you now desire to occupy and to the degree that you are self-persuaded, you will enter it. Don't believe in anyone outside of your own wonderful human imagination! Every coin is inscribed with the statement: "In God we trust" yet I wonder how many trust in God . . and not the coin! If you really believe in God (I AM), you can be penniless, yet walk in the assumption of wealth and be wealthy. Learn to trust your own wonderful human imagination, for he is the only God. Do that and you will never go wrong!

It is well to remember that the enlightened in every age have taught that back of all things there is One Unseen Cause: In studying the teachings of the great thinkers we find that a common thread runs through all--the thread of Unity. There is no record of any deep thinker, of any age, who taught duality. One of the great teachings of Moses was, "Hear, O Israel, the Lord our God is One Lord"; and the saying, "I AM that I AM," was old when Moses was yet unborn; for it had been inscribed over the temple entrances for generations. We may go back much farther than Moses and find the same teaching, for it crops out from the literatures and sayings of the wise of all ages. Jesus taught this when He said, "I and the Father are One," and in the saying, "The Father that dwelleth in me." This teaching of Unity is the chief cornerstone of the Sacred Scriptures of the East as well as of our own Sacred Writings. It is today the mainspring of the teachings of the modern philosophies, such as Christian Science, Divine Science, The Unity Teachings, The New Thought Movement, The Occult Teachings, The Esoteric or Inner Teachings, and even of much that is taught under the name of Psychology. Without this basic teaching of Unity these movements would have but little to offer. Science has found nothing to contradict this teaching, and it never will, for the teaching is self-evident.

Who are you but that unknown power of the Eternal whom no man hath seen or comprehended fully? You are that One coming to consciousness, awakening to the realization of yourself, and just beginning to know and feel that the power of the Almighty is yours to manifest for the good of all. You are growing to Godhood through exerting the power that is inherently yours. The Being of God is your Being, the foundation for all that you are, and God is glorified in glorifying you. Who else shall he glorify but Himself made manifest? Awake! Arise! Proclaim your own Being the King of your nature and of your world. Assert your I AM in the quality of divine love and you will add a positive pole to your mental battery that will make you a mighty magnet, holding subject to your will all the less developed and negative forces of your nature. You can realize by constant practice that your will is the focal point for the mighty energies of God.

The name Jehovah-jireh means "Jehovah will see," "Jehovah will behold," "Jehovah will provide." It signifies "I AM the provider." If we expect to demonstrate prosperity from without, we find it a slow process; but if we know that the I AM is the provider, we have the key to the inexhaustible resource.

When we speak of the Universal Mind, we mean the Omnipresent Consciousness of God, the One Mind which inheres in all things, whose activity is Universal. Omnipresence completely fills the Universe. Everything is filled with the Principle of Life. Since His consciousness is our consciousness, we lack nothing. Mind is everywhere; there is no place where God is not. Man is a conscious, willing, thinking, knowing center of the Universal Mind of God. The I AM reacts to him according to the sum total of his beliefs. Man is Universal on the subjective side of life, and individual at the point of conscious perception. The individual uses the creative power of the Universal Mind every time he uses his own mind. Mind is everywhere, in everything and through everything: everything can respond to our thought. Jesus revealed this Truth when He spoke to the fig tree, saying, Bear no more fruit, henceforth; when He spoke to the winds and commanded them to be peaceful. When a unity has been established between the individual and the Universal I AM, Mind Substance can be directed into any channel. The Universal Mind is always impersonal. It never decides who shall use it. It becomes personal only as It expresses through us. It doesn't matter who we are, or what we are. The sun shines on the good and the evil, and the rain falls on the just and the unjust. God is accessible and responsive to all. Cast thy bread upon the waters, for thou shalt find it after many days. The Law is exact. Thoughts are things, and things are thoughts. Cast your thought into the Universal Mind, and in due time it will return as form.

The feet symbolize our understanding. When we die to our false beliefs and superstitions, we are ready to believe that the God-Presence (I AM) is none other than our consciousness or awareness. Our consciousness is without face, form, or figure. It is the Invisible, Formless Power within us, taking form according to our thought and feeling. Here in your world of the mind or consciousness, you are the Christ or King of your world. Your robe as a king is the garment or mood of love. The crown you wear is the awareness of the Power of God (I AM). The scepter you hold is your authority to use this Power to bless, heal, and inspire.

The I AM affirmation or suggestion is one of tremendous power. In the realization of Oneness with the Infinite, one may affirm with conviction "I AM" . . whatever is affirmative and constructive, whatever is representative of Truth or Principle, whatever is of the quality or attribute of the Infinite. That one does not at the time manifest the ideal that is affirmed is not inconsistent with the statement, while one's absorption of the ideal tends to transmute it from the realm of Being to that of physical form.

To develop individuality, the first essential is to give the "I AM" its true and lofty position in your mind. The "I AM" is the very center of individuality, and the more fully conscious you become of the "I AM" the more of the power that is in the "I AM" you arouse, and it is the arousing of this power that makes individuality positive and strong. Another essential is to practice the idea of feeling or conceiving yourself as occupying the masterful attitude. Whenever you think of yourself, think of yourself as being and living and acting in the masterful attitude. Then in addition, make every desire positive, make every feeling positive, make every thought positive, and make every action of mind positive.

"Now do I have that serene consciousness that is sure of the fact that thought controls substance and passes it out into form. Now do I feel, deep within my being, that the things I desire shall come to pass. I not only know that these things can be but that they will be. I am conscious of the fact that I and the Father are one. He is creative; I AM creative: He is changeless substance; I AM changeless substance: He is eternal; I AM eternal: He is perfect; I AM perfect: He is complete; I AM complete. As He creates by thinking, so do I. I am conscious of myself as self directing. I have faith; I believe in the power of my own word to bring things forth out of the invisible."

The entire 15th chapter of the Book of John is devoted to this pruning of the vine. He starts off: "I AM the true vine. My Father is the vinedresser. Every branch of mine that bears no fruit he prunes, that it may bear more fruit." The tree in your garden may be lovely to look at and it may pain you to cut a certain branch, but you know you must do it if you want good fruit next year. That is life. Consciousness (the I AM) is the eternal vine. Your eternal body is the Imagination, which is God himself. We are all members of the divine body . . Jesus; therefore humanity is truly the body of the Lord Jesus Christ. Every child is part of that universal body; and when he knows that Jesus Christ (I AM) is his own wonderful human imagination, he is confused for the moment, until the realization rearranges itself within him. Then he takes himself in hand, determined to do something about it. I tell you from experience, if you will take yourself in hand and really believe in Christ (I AM) in you to the point that you will turn to no other causation, but will prune your thoughts morning, noon, and night, your world will change. It will mold itself in harmony with the change which has taken place in you, for your outer world is forever reflecting your inner, imaginal acts.

All causes are more positive than their effects. All the forces of life and intelligence of which the mighty Mind of God consults are positive, more positive than electricity, even more positive than the mind of humanity. Your mind must be tuned to supreme positiveness if you would realize the power of life. Your faith in the power of life to overcome every negative condition must be more positive than your belief in the lack of life and health if you would polarize the intelligent healing power of the divine life. Electricity flows freely through the copper wire, but when it meets the positive resistance of the wire in the glass bulb it instantly generates heat and light. The electricity glorifies that which is as positive as itself. Life will glorify you with its power of health and perfection as your faith becomes as positive as life. You will become Godlike with divine powers as you develop in the strength of I AM-ness which polarizes and radiates the life, intelligence and love of the universal Father to all. Always remember that one of the conditions of divine receptivity is humility toward the supreme Power. The most Godlike realize that their strength is the strength of the Father. As the friction between the electricity and the resistant wire generates light and heat, so the vibration of the wonderful forces of the universal mind against the positive center of your mind will generate the heat of divine love and the light of true wisdom which will make you a mighty power for good, a radiant center of all the divine attributes that you have developed.

The most inclusive name for Being is Jehovah God. Jehovah represents the individual I AM and God (Elohim) the universal Principle. When man thinks or says "I AM" he is potentially giving freedom to the seed ideas that contains in its spiritual capacity all of Being. The natural man in his narrowed mental comprehension barely touches the seed ideas that expand in the Christ man to infinite power. The more we dwell upon and expand our I AM the greater looms its originating capacity before us. When Jesus proclaimed, "Before Abraham, was I AM," He realized that the I AM preceded all manifestation, however great, and was capable of infinite expression.

The universal Substance with which you are working in the Silence is the most sensitive Substance in the world. In its native state, it is unformed, but It solidifies or assumes any form possible to your belief. It distributes Itself through the visual power of your mind. The I AM sends its Substance into the picture that the directive power of yours will give. You use your will to train the imagination to see only those things which you wish to experience. The quickest way to blot out an adverse or disastrous thought is to ask yourself this question: Is this what I want to happen?

Before any manifestation appears, it must first come out of the invisible. We must first have the feeling of conviction in our own consciousness. Where were you before you were born? You are told in plain language you were in the I AM state. You were in the Absolute or Paradisiacal State. When your boy or girl is born, the child is the Universal Life, God, or I AM assuming the role of that particular child. It is the Unconditioned becoming conditioned. It is the Formless taking form. "I was naked and ye clothed me."

Whenever you exercise the will, try to place the action of that will as deeply in the world of your interior mental feeling as you possibly can; that is, do not originate will-action on the surface, but in the depth of your own supreme individuality. Try to feel that it is the "I AM" that is exercising the power of the will, and then remember that the "I AM" lives constantly upon the supreme heights of absolute self-mastery. With this inspiring thought constantly in mind, you will carry the throne of the will, so to speak, farther and farther back into the interior realms of your greater mental world, higher and higher up into the ruling power of the supreme principle in mind. The result will be that you will steadily increase the power of your will, and appropriate more and more the conscious control of that principle in your greater nature through which all the forces in your possession may be governed and directed.

So don't let anything that has happened in your life discourage you. Don't let poverty or lack of education or past failures hold you back. There is only one power . . the I AM in you . . and it can do anything. If in the past you have not used that power, that is too bad as far as the past is concerned, but it is not too late. You can start NOW. "Be still, and know that I AM God." What more are you waiting for? God can do for you only what you allow Him to do through you, but if you will do your part, He can use you as a channel for unlimited power and good. The difference between failure and success is measured only by your patience and faith . . sometimes by inches, sometimes by minutes, sometimes by the merest flash of time.

In the 64th chapter of the Book of Isaiah we read: "O Lord, thou art our Father; we are the clay. Thou art our potter; we are the work of thy hand." When you hear the words Lord, Father, and potter, do you think of another? I certainly hope not. The word "Lord" is Jod He Vau He [pron. "Yod Hey Vav Hey"] which is defined as "I AM". Your own wonderful I AMness is the Lord, your Father. And the word "potter" means "imagination; that which is shaping your world." Imagination is the Lord, the potter, the shaper of your world, molding it into its present form.

The central and most vital fact that they must come to realize is that an idea has the power of building thought structures, which in turn materialize in the outer environment and affairs and determine every detail of their existence. Every man is a king ruling his own subjects. These subjects are the ideas existing in his mind, the "subjects" of his thought. Each man's ideas are as varied and show as many traits of character as the inhabitants of any empire. But they can all be brought into subjection and made to obey through the I AM power that is the ruler of the kingdom. In your domain of mind there may be colonies of alien ideas . . the Philistines, Canaanites, and other foreign tribes, that the Children of Israel found in their Promised Land when they attempted to take possession of it. The story of the Children of Israel and how they gained the possession of that land is a symbolical representation of the experience of everyone who seeks to reclaim his own consciousness in the name of the Lord. The meaning in Hebrew of the name Canaanite is "merchant" or "trader"; in other words, a set of ideas that has to do with the commercial phase of life. Study the Children of Israel (spiritual ideas) in their experiences with these Canaanites and you will get many valuable hints on subduing and handling your own money-getting ideas.

Be ye transformed by the renewing of your mind. The Truth can only be known as the entire consciousness is surrendered to the Universal Mind which is Oneness, Wholeness and Completeness. The Law must be fulfilled in our consciousness by the clear perception that God is all. Merely thinking the Truth never changes anyone. It is the conscious knowing of the Truth that changes man from a material to a spiritual basis. Knowing the Truth means to have the true idea of Principle or God and the true idea of man. The word Principle used so frequently in our lessons means the Law of God . . the I AM, Universal Mind, Spiritual Substance, the Omnipresent, Omnipotence and Omniscience of our own Minds. One cannot think of the word Principle without losing the thought of the personal. Since the true nature of God is impersonal, the word will gradually clear the concept of a personal God subject to all the limitations which personality connotes.

"Whom seek ye" means that we are always seeking Jesus, or the thing that would save us. The only way we can receive our good is on the basis of our understanding of the laws of mind and our consciousness of complete acceptance. The voice answered, "I AM He."

This world is the sphere of the "I AM"; in other words, that state of being wherein you become actually conscious of the great truth that "I AM" is identical with you. When you can clearly think of yourself as "I AM," and can actually feel that "I AM" is neither mind nor body, soul nor spirit, but is above all of these in the most supreme state of individualized being, you are beginning to enter within the sacred domains of absolute truth. Affirm as frequently as possible the statement, I AM THE REAL I AM, and try to realize, whenever you make that statement, that "I AM" is the reigning power in your being; that "I AM" is God individualized in your being; that "I AM" is the only begotten Son, the Christ enthroned in your being; and that "I AM" actually is the "real you" of your being. You thus not only recognize the supreme position of "I AM," but you also recognize yourself as being "I AM"; you lift your consciousness of yourself out of "material thought" into the pure light of spiritual thought; you find your real self and you discover that you . . the real you, the whole of you, reigns on high, where all life is forever in purity, health, power, freedom, truth; you become conscious of yourself in the world of supreme spiritual consciousness, and your eyes are opened in "another and a better world," to the great truth that you are, here and now, not only the likeness of God, but the individualized spirit of God. You find that the only difference between the "I AM" that is you and the "I AM That I AM," is that the former is individualized while the latter is infinite.

In short, when you say or think "I AM," you are conscious of the existence of your real self, and feel the growth of a new sense of power within you. This recognition of the self may be but faint; but encourage it and it will grow, and whilst growing will manifest itself to your mind by impressing upon the latter the knowledge of the proper plan for further development. It is an example of "to him who hath shall be given, and to him who hath not shall be taken away even that which he hath." The mere calling of the attention to the fact may awaken the recognition in some, whilst others will find it necessary to reflect upon the idea and awaken to a recognition of the truth more slowly. Some will not feel the truth. To such I say: The time is not yet ripe for your recognition of this great truth, but the seed is planted and the plant will appear in time. This may seem like the veriest nonsense to you now, but the time will come when you will admit its literal correctness. To those who feel the first indications of the awakening of the real self, I say: Carry the thought with you and it will unfold like the lotus, naturally and gradually; the truth once recognized cannot be lost, and there is no standing still in nature. To those who recognize the truth, I would like to say more, but this is not the place.

Difficulties may beset you, obstacles get in your way, and ill health hold you down. Bless them! Know that there is only one God (I AM) and He is good, therefore anything evil that may trouble you is GOOD in disguise. You have heard the old aphorism that . . "When Fortune means to man most good; she looks upon him with a threatening eye." If you can bless every seeming evil, know that it is really Good working for you in another guise and that it is working with all else of life for your own good, it will quickly show you the silver lining underneath. It is only as you RESIST evil that it turns to harm.

You can be the man (or woman) you want to be, but not by simply wishing. You must make the effort to look at the world mentally and see it reflect your fulfilled desire. And when it does you must remain in that state until you reach the inner conviction that what you are seeing, touching, tasting, smelling, and hearing is true, clothe yourself in the feeling of its reality . . and explode! Do that and you are pregnant. And what do you do after pregnancy? Nothing! You simply wait for its birth to appear in its own appointed hour. And it will! When you least expect it your desire will objectify itself in the world for you to enjoy, whether it be health, wealth, or fame. That's how God's (I AM) law works.

By make positive affirmations, we can enable the I AM to grow more vibrant and alive. We can then aspire to know and to do more of the goodwill of the Creator. This exercise of goodwill links our I AM more closely with the Angel Hosts. We are learning to exalt our thoughts and will into the same state as that of the Angel Hosts. But we could not bring that thought and power out from the interior sufficiently to change the lower qualities of our brains and overcome the spirits which vibrated to those lower qualities. Our brains were clouded with qualities of thought and feeling which placed us in rapport with spirits of like quality. Even after we aspired to conquer these hereditary qualities of mind, they remained because they were strengthened by the influx of the same spiritual quality from spirits who desired to hold our minds subject to their ancient beliefs and debilitating desires. This clouding of the brain shows why the Divinity in humanity has been smothered and kept in subjection. As long as humanity believes that the Creator was separate from them, and that God had to be propitiated to save them, their own Divinity would have no power to rise up and throw off materiality and selfishness, and overthrow the spirits of deception.

Start now to put your imagination to the test. Jesus Christ is in you and you will not fail if you call your desire forth with God's name. Sleep in the assumption that you already are the person you desire to be, and firmly expect the evidence to appear in your world. The last bold statement in the Book of John is: "I AM the true vine." If God's name is I AM and it is synonymous with God Himself, then I . . the vine . . will grow and produce the fruit I AM aware of. If you dare to remain conscious of any state, it must appear! Claim for yourself that which you would like to experience. Then put your hope fully upon the grace that is coming to you at the unveiling of Christ within you.

When the first act takes place, count the days, and you will discover the last act will appear exactly 1,260 days later. After that, you will linger to tell your story to those who will listen. Not everyone will, for they are interested only in things of this world. Show them how to get their things until they hunger for the promise. Then Christ will unveil himself in them and they will discover they are God the Father. Yes, I AM the way, the truth, the life, and the vine. But when I come to the end, I AM the Father.

Spirit knows Itself, but the Law is the servant of the Spirit and is set in motion through Its Word. It is known that all law is some form of universal force or energy. Law does not know itself; law only knows to do; it is, therefore, the servant of the Spirit. It is the way that the Spirit works; and is the medium through which It operates to fulfill Its purpose.

Did God (I AM) make law? As it is not possible to conceive a time when law did not operate, it is impossible to conceive that it was ever created; therefore, law must be coexistent and co-eternal with Spirit. We might say that law is one of the attributes of Spirit.

The Spirit operates through law which is some part of Its own Nature; therefore, all action must be some action of Spirit as Law. The Word of Spirit sets Its purposes in motion through the law; and since the law must be as Infinite as the Spirit, we could not think of a time when it was not, or a time when it would cease to be; neither can we imagine the law ever failing to operate when set in motion.

We have, then, an Infinite Spirit and an Infinite Law; Intelligence and the way that It works; God (I AM), working through Law, which is unfailing and certain.

We should not fail to think always of the spiritual law under which the I AM moves. It is possible for man to take I AM power and apply it in external ways and leave out the true spiritual law. In our day we are proclaiming that man can use I AM power to restore health and bring increased happiness; in fact, that through righteous, lawful use of the I AM he can have everything that he desires. But some people are using this power in a material way, neglecting soul culture, building up the external without taking the intermediate step between the supreme Mind and its manifestation in the outer. We should remember that the soul must grow as well as the body.

As long as thoughts of self and of the things of the world are dominant in the mind, the mind is in touch only with the mortal vibration of the earth plane. It is constantly drawing that quality of vibration of which it is in the habit of thinking. It may say over and over "I AM the love of God" but unless it is lifted out of the mortal sphere of thought at the same time and feels the love of God while thinking the thought, it has no more effect than any intellectual exercise.

"Thoughts are things" and occupy space in the mind realm. They have substance and form and may easily be taken as permanent by one not endowed with spiritual discernment. They bring forth fruit according to the seed planted in the mind, but they are not enduring unless founded in Spirit. Thoughts are alive and are endowed by the thinker with a secondary thinking power; that is, the thought entity that the I AM forms assumes an ego and begins to think on its own account. Thoughts also think but only with the power you give to them. Tell me what kind of thoughts you are holding about yourself and your neighbors, and I can tell you just what you may expect in the way of health, finances, and harmony in your home. Are you suspicious of your neighbors? You cannot love and trust in God if you hate and distrust men. The two ideas love and hate, or trust and mistrust, simply cannot both be present in your mind at one time, and when you are entertaining one, you may be sure the other is absent. Trust other people and use the power that you accumulate from that act to trust God. There is magic in it: it works wonders; love and trust are dynamic, vital powers. Are you accusing men of being thieves, and fear that they are going to take away from you something that is your own? With such a thought generating fear and even terror in your mind and filling your consciousness with darkness, where is there room for the Father's light of protection? Rather build walls of love and substance around yourself. Send out swift, invisible messengers of love and trust for your protection.

This creative power is buried in everyone, and that power is God himself. There is no intermediary between you and God. Jesus Christ is the creative power of your own wonderful human imagination! That is Jesus Christ and there is no other! God the Father is buried in you as your I AM, and your human I AMness is Jesus Christ. This is the being Paul speaks of when he says: "Test yourself; Do you not realize that Jesus Christ is in you? Unless, of course, you fail to meet the test." Now let me share a letter from a friend. She said: "I am a freelance designer. I never seek work, but as I sit at home and imagine I am working, they call. In the past six months I have received very few orders from a company that kept me very busy in the past, so I called them to discover that they had employed a full-time art director and would no longer require my services. After hanging up the phone I revised this conversation. I heard them tell me they had lots of work for me, and I felt the thrill in their words. One week later they called, asking me to design a 26-page book of institutional advertising, plus four ads for Harper's Bazaar. This was more than they had given me in the past at any one time. Now I am busier, happier, and making more money than ever before, and my technique is simple. Sitting in my chair I quietly listen for the phone to ring, answer it in my imagination and hear the orders I desire to create . . and they come."

Having come to the recognition of the truth that I AM all mind, that every cell of my body has the capacity for intelligent action and is responsive to my will, I desire to cultivate this latent mind of my flesh so that my will shall be done throughout my whole mental organization. How shall I proceed? The animal is an undeveloped and transitional form of the mind that reaches a higher state of development in humanity. Now that we have attained to maturity, with self-conscious understanding of our possibilities as mental creatures, let us lay aside the propensities and the selfish habits of animals for the full enjoyment and expansion of our mental powers. Until humanity has gained conscious dominion over the animal propensities and turned all the sexual force into mental power obedient to its will, it has not become initiated into the real enjoyment of life nor has it made conditions for the permanent health of its body. Perfect health of body, as well as the continual regeneration of the tissues, to the sublimation of old age, is possible for all by the application of this principle of the conservation of vital energy, along with the conscious control of the organs by the will.

Until we function consciously in and from the Soul, until we act from the Self in which all power resides, we shall be unable to control our forces. The masterful individuality which speaks from the soul is the Supreme Self, or I AM of God. This I AM is always conscious of Itself. It responds to the man outside as he responds to It. Spirit knows man only at the level of his ability to know himself. Through the spirit (I AM), we can in the Silence establish a means of communion between the man outside and the Man Inside. Each one of us must contact God through his own mind until He takes possession of our consciousness. The secret of spiritual power is the individual consciousness of union with God. The I AM is Good. It is Love, Life, Law Intelligence and Power, but it interprets Itself to man only as he mentally embodies the whole, only as he recognizes the I AM as the changeless Principle of his own mind. The more completely he becomes conscious of this union, the more power and dominion he expresses. Health, harmony, happiness and prosperity are effects, not causes.

Christ is the subjective Wisdom and Power of God (I AM) which you call forth when you still your mind and reject the appearance of things. As you quietly contemplate the answer, you become aware of the Inner Voice and Divine Wisdom which wells up and anoints your intellect, showing you the way you should go.

God (I AM) speaks to man only through the medium of his basic desires. Your desires are determined by your conception of yourself. Of themselves they are neither good or evil. "I know and am persuaded by the Lord Christ Jesus that there is nothing unclean of itself but to him that seeth anything to be unclean to him it is unclean." Your desires are the natural and automatic result of your present conception of yourself. God (I AM), your unconditioned consciousness, is impersonal and no respecter of persons. Your unconditioned consciousness, God (I AM), gives to your conditioned consciousness, man, through the medium of your basic desires that which your conditioned state (your present conception of yourself) believes it needs. As long as you remain in your present conscious state so long will you continue desiring that which you now desire. Change your conception of yourself and you will automatically change the nature of your desires. Desires are states of consciousness seeking embodiment. They are formed by man's consciousness and can easily be expressed by the man who has conceived them. Desires are expressed when the man who has conceived them assumes the attitude of mind that would be his if the states desired were already expressed.

In the Book of Romans, the 4th chapter, the 17th verse, Paul tells us: "God calls things that are not seen as though they were seen and the unseen becomes seen." How does he do it? By the act of movement. I move and that which was invisible becomes visible. I see you now, but you have told me your desire. It is invisible, but by the act of movement I can see your face radiantly happy because your desire has now taken on life and substance. I have moved, and in so doing I see you differently. Now, if I move from that I AM into what I would like to be, you will still be my friend; so in my imagination I let you see me as you would have to see me if things were as I want them to be, and there I remain. I can't be double-minded and let you see me in my former state, but must persist in my new state until it becomes natural and out pictures itself in my world. This is true of everything you do, I don't care what it is. If you want to be known, you will be, regardless of the fact that you start your assumption with nothing to support your claim. Simply dare to assume that you are, for your assumptions . . although denied by your senses . . if persisted in will become externalized facts in your life.

Thus there is but one Principle, uniform in all its operations in all religions and in no religion. Without understanding men have unconsciously obeyed the Law. That Law is found in the Principle of Concentration in sincerity upon the ideal. This is but another way of saying "I AM THAT WHICH I THINK I AM!" I pray, thinking I have received, and lo! I have received. Thus prayer is a common and instinctive method of arriving at health, happiness and success through Concentration.

Tennyson tells us "More things are wrought by prayer than this world dreams of," because through prayer the Principle of Concentration is applied to daily living. When the Law is understood and practiced by you, you will have found the only way in which conscious man has directed his development. He has wrought through the concentration as Will. upon that thought which is born of desire. Any form of prayer which one sincerely uses, will work the end which is desired in the Thought expressed. Thoughts are materialized into life through prayer.

Mental activity in Divine Mind represents two phases: first, conception of the idea; and secondly, expression of the idea. In every idea conceived in mind there is first the quickening spirit of life, followed by the increase of the idea in substance. Wisdom is the "male" or expressive side of Being, while love is the "female" or receptive side of Being. Wisdom is the father quality of God and love is the mother quality. In every idea there exist these two qualities of mind, which unite in order to increase and bring forth under divine law. Divine Mind blessed the union of wisdom and love and pronounced on them the increase of Spirit. When wisdom and love are unified in the individual consciousness, man is a master of ideas and brings forth under the original creative law. "Seed" represents fundamental ideas having within themselves reproductive capacity. Every idea is a seed that, sown in the substance of mind, becomes the real food on which man is nourished. Man has access to the seed ideas of Divine Mind, and through prayer and meditation he quickens and appropriates the substance of those ideas, which were originally planted in his I AM by the parent mind.

AMEN! Jesus concluded the prayer with the oldest word in our possession. Amen. The word is actually the sacred name for the Power back of all creation and means literally, The Hidden One. Amen is really the cohesive force of any prayer. It is a word that precipitates immediate expression. It clinches and vitalizes all other affirmations. It sets the Universal Forces into activity. Amen should be used after every affirmation and prayer, and be thought of as the Power of the I AM (Spirit) to impregnate substance. Amen is the mighty pronouncement that It is done.

Let us take the following simple illustration: A man wishes to be healed and affirms over and over, "I AM healed." If his statements are mechanical, he will get no results. He must enter into the spirit or feeling of perfect health. He must claim and feel the truth of what he affirms in consciousness. Healing follows the silent inner knowing of the soul. To be wealthy I must assume the consciousness of wealth; then wealth will follow. If you want to grow spiritually, there is a wonderful standard set up by Paul, Whatsoever things are honest, whatsoever things are just, whatsoever things are pure, whatsoever things are lovely, whatsoever things are of good report; if there be any virtue, and if there be any praise, think on these things.

To further prove the Law of obedience, the steam that wrecks the train is the same good old steam that carries the train in safety, only the ignorance of someone using it is at fault. Steam itself is obedient to the manipulator of it and can only act as directed. Take exactly the same attitude toward the Power within (I AM) and direct It where you desire It to manifest, only, unlike steam, the Power within is great enough to hold worlds in space, and you wield this Power every time you think. Do not direct It to hold you in debt any longer, but think, rather, I AM free, and rest assured It will act as your freedom. You thus become not only free yourself, but you will also aid in freeing everyone else from a belief of debt; for the great reservoir of subconscious mind of which you are a part, or rather with which you are one, carries in ever-widening circles the truth you voice to all who are receptive to truth.

I AM is the key to scripture. Called Jesus Christ in the New Testament, God the Father's name is revealed in the Old Testament as I AM. Having come into the world to fulfill the word, you cannot return empty but must accomplish that which you purposed and prosper in the thing for which you sent yourself. After inspiring the prophets to tell your story, you came not only to fulfill their prophecy, but to share your experiences to encourage others.

The Great "I AM." . . Revealed to Moses as the One and Only Real Mind or Power in the Universe. That beside Which there is no other. I AM is another way of saying God. The "I AM" in man is the Life of man; without this "I AM," man could not be. Conscious Mind . . That Power of Consciousness which knows Itself. That which is conscious of Its Own Being. "The Spirit is the power Which knows Itself." The Self-Knowing God. The Intelligence in the Universe which reveals Itself in all of Its Creation. If God were not Self-Conscious, then man could not be self-conscious. It is impossible for us to conceive of such a Universal Consciousness. We touch It only in spots, but the evidence of this Conscious Mind is strewn throughout all time and space; and the eternal activity of the Cosmos is proof enough that such a Conscious Mind really exists.

To reach a higher level of being, you must assume a higher concept of yourself. If you will not imagine yourself as other than what you are, then you remain as you are, "for if ye believe not that I AM He, ye shall die in your sins." If you do not believe that you are He, the person you want to be, then you remain as you are. Through the faithful systematic cultivation of the feeling of the wish fulfilled, desire becomes the promise of its own fulfillment. The assumption of the feeling of the wish fulfilled makes the future dream a present fact.

By affirming your own Being in the Name, I AM, you will make yourself positive as a receiver and generator of the Positive Power of Divine Mind. And, vibrating together to the Tone of the Divine I AM, we shall help each other to attune the world to Divine Thought. We share the results and benefits of our years of concentration and realization with you. These principles will help open the Door for you so that you may realize greater life and energy: and as you study and practice with us, you will learn to appropriate this energy and to organize it into your own personality as health, joy and prosperity. We urge you to recognize that your good is to come through your own spirit, by practicing the Method which has done so much for all who have applied its principles.

Start examining yourself. Do you believe that imagining creates reality? If you do, then test yourself. Do you not realize that Jesus Christ (imagination) is in you? Do you have the courage to claim; "I AM He and besides me there is no other?" In the 8th chapter of John, the statement is made: "You will die in your sins unless you believe that I AM He." This is not a statement of another telling you that you must believe he is God. No! You are forever talking to yourself! Limited by the five senses, "I" . . Christ (Imagination) in you . . will miss my goals in life unless "I" believe that "I AM" that which "I" formerly desired to be.

Jesus Christ is God (I AM) himself, who became you, individually. Your awareness is He. When you imagine, God (I AM) is acting. He is the true vine and the vinedresser, for he is your imagination, imagining you. If you really understand this, you will start pruning your thoughts. If you don't and continue to believe Jesus Christ is other than your Self, you will persist in allowing your wanton energy to run wild, to swell into irregular twigs, and bear unlovely things in your world. When you become aware of those in need, even though you do not know them personally, do you use your imagination to lift them from that state? That is what you are called upon to do.

If you represent them to yourself as you would like them to be, and persuade yourself it is true, that branch will change in your world. You do not eliminate the state of need. It remains for anyone to be aware of, but you . . having lifted yourself out of the state . . see it no more. Prune your vine morning, noon, and night; and then . . when you least expect it . . a series of wonderful, supernatural experiences will be yours, as God reveals himself in you . . not as another, but as your very Self. Then you will say, from personal experience, "I AM He."

The name Eve means "elemental life," "life," "living." Eve represents the soul region of man and is the mother principle of God in expression through which life is evolved. The I AM (wisdom) puts feeling into what it thinks, and so Eve (feeling) becomes the "mother of all living." Back of feeling is the pure life essence of God. Adam and Eve symbolize the I AM individualized in life and substance. They are the primal elemental forces of Being itself.

Start now to use your talent, which is your imagination. Use it consciously every day, for any time you use your imagination you are pleasing God (I AM); and when you do not use it God (I AM) is displeased. You don't have to sit down and burst a blood vessel pounding out the details of your desire. You can imagine as you walk down the street. A simple assumption is easy and can be lots of fun. A friend called today to thank me for aiding her in the selling of her home. It was an enormous house in Highland Park, which had been empty for some time. She had hired a lady to go to the house and do some cleaning there, when a man came to the door and asked to buy it. Two weeks later the house was sold. What did I do? I imagined hearing her tell me the house was sold. That's all I did. There was nothing else I needed to do; for all things are possible to God (I AM), and he so loves me he abides by any request I make of him.

It is very important for us to know that we grow like that which we study. If we keep before our minds the beauty and perfection which the Ever-Present Great Spirit has bestowed upon all of creation, we will find our souls attracted more and more to that divine ideal, until the same love which our Creator has for all creation will be kindled within us, and we shall know that we are all brothers and sisters in oneness with the same Ever-Presence. The most perfect and permanent healing is attained only by the perception of this grand truth and the awakening of the soul to the realization of the mighty love of the I AM. This Love must endow us with a feeling of universal fellowship with all souls as children of the one Creator; we must feel toward all just as the Great Spirit feels toward us, if we would be healed by this transforming love. The Ever-Present Intelligence yearns to heal and prosper all souls, but unless It can find entrance and expression through our souls as love, Its power is limited so far as we are concerned.

When He, the Spirit of truth, has come, he will guide you into all truth. The Spirit of Truth is the I AM of the Universal Mind. When man recognizes that his consciousness is One with the I AM Consciousness, the recognition will guide him into all Truth. We cannot change the truth, but we can change the manifestation of the Law.

God is "I AM" and "I AM" God. When the personal mind (conscious) relaxes and "lets" the great Mind (I AM) at the center of one's very Being express, it will work and work perfectly. As you recall the teaching step by step, you will be aware that "I AM" is at the center of things. You also find that "I AM" is at the center of your own Being. This then is plain and reasonable . . that when you are still and your conscious mind is conscious not of things. but of the "I AM" within you, you are in tune with everything in the Universe. Being in tune with the Universe, you exert an unconscious pull on things and will draw to you the thing which you desire most. That is why I do not say, "Think of the thing that you want," but "Think of the Substance (I AM) of the thing." This great Universal Mind (I AM) is always flowing into our bodies, whether we are conscious of it or not.

God is the true vine, for I AM means God, and all men are rooted in God or Life. For example, every man is rooted in you, since life gives birth to all of us. The Life-Principle is One and Indivisible. It was never born and it will never die. We receive our life, our strength, and substance from God (I AM). His Life is our life; His Power is our power. It is the one Being appearing as the many. Look to the God-Presence within for your thoughts, guidance, and health. Feel and know you are rooted in the Divine from whom all blessings flow.

Test my words, for I know the human imagination is God. Call forth your desire by calling it forth with God's name. Decide what you want and ask yourself what it would be like and how you would feel if it were true. Then dare to assume you have it. Let the people who know you now see you after your assumption. Don't make them see you; let them see the change! Think of the world as a sounding box, echoing and reflecting what you have assumed. Listen to your friends comment on your change. See their faces expressing their pleasure on your good fortune. Wear that feeling as you now wear your present body of belief. Continue to wear that new state and in no time at all your desire will objectify itself and become a fact in your world. Then you will know who the cause of the phenomena of life really is. There is only one source. The world calls it God. That is a lovely name, but don't forget that God is your awareness! No one can see I AM!

We are constantly affirming our way through life; and since affirmation is the only mental action possible, it behooves us to find the greatest affirmation and use it. The Supreme Affirmation is, "I AM"; and, as such, It was given to Moses. This affirmation is constantly with us, and every time we speak we use it in some form. We must be careful to use it only as an upbuilding force.

Leave the good and evil and eat of the Tree of Life.
Nothing in the world is untrue if you want it to be true. You are the truth of everything that you perceive. "I AM the truth, and the way, the life revealed." If I have physically nothing in my pocket, then in Imagination I have MUCH. But that is a lie based on fact, but truth is based on the intensity of my imagination and then I will create it in my world. Should I accept facts and use them as to what I should imagine? No.

It is told us in the story of the fig tree. It did not bear for three years. One said, "Cut it down, and throw it away." But the keeper of the vineyard pleaded NO! Who is the tree? I AM the tree; you are the tree. We bear or we do not. But the Keeper said he would dig around the tree and feed it . . or manure it, as we would say today . . and see if it will not bear. Well I do that here every week and try to get the tree . . you . . me to bear. You should bear whatever you desire. If you want to be happily married, you should be. The world is only response. If you want money, get it. Everything is a dream anyway. When you awake and know what you are creating and that you are creating it that is a different thing.

If man knew that his Awareness was God, and that his desire was simply life urging him forward, he would turn within to the Source (I AM) and claim his desire as a reality now.

The I AM is your real self. When your mind recognizes its master, you will have learned the secret of Life. I have planted this thought seed in your mind, and it will grow and evolve into a beautiful plant bearing a flower whose fragrance will surpass that of earth's fairest blossoms. When its leaves unfold and show the flower in all its beauty, then will you know that you have found yourself. "I AM" is eternal, and impregnable to harm. It is powerful, and, when the mind has learned to adapt itself to its influence, man becomes like another being, and acquires hitherto unknown powers.

"I can of Mine Own Self do nothing . . because I seek not Mine Own Will, but the Will of the Father which hath sent Me." In this quotation, the Father obviously refers to God. In an earlier chapter, God is defined as I AM. Since creation is finished, the Father is never in a position of saying "I will be".

In other words, everything exists, and the infinite I AM consciousness can speak only in the present tense. "Not My Will, but Thine be done." "I will be" is a confession that "I AM not". The Father's Will is always "I AM". Until you realize that you are the Father (there is only one I AM, and your infinite self is that I AM), your will is always "I will be".

Self-Existent . . It is difficult to grasp the idea of self-existence; but we can do so to a degree at least. For instance, we might ask the question, "Why is water wet?" There is no reason why; it is wet simply because it is its nature to be wet. If we were to ask the question, "Who made Life?", it could not be answered; because if we were to assume that some power made Life we would not be supposing that Life is First Cause. We must grasp the fact that, in dealing with Real Being, we are dealing with that which was never created. When did two times two begin to make four? Never, of course. It is a self-existent truth. God did not make God; God is. This is the meaning of the saying, "I AM THAT I AM." All inquiry into Truth must begin with the self-evident fact that Life Is. The Truth is that which Is and so is Self-Existent.

Man is all Imagination, and God is man and exists in us and we in him. The eternal body of man is the Imagination and that is God himself, the divine body of Jesus. And we, on the surface, are his master. All are the members of this one divine body and only this one body, all gathered into the unity in the one body, which is God. Call it God or Jehovah, or Jesus Christ or I AM. You can say I AM or Imagination in a group like this that understands and get behind names and surfaces. But in the outer world I wouldn't use it because they wouldn't understand.

I AM is the spiritual name of Jehovah, the ever-living one. When we affirm, "I AM," with our thoughts centered on Spirit, we quicken the life flow in the body and awaken the sleepy cells. Such affirmations clear up congested areas of the organism and restore the circulation to its normal state, health. A prominent scientist recently stated that man's body is composed of trillions of cells, every one an electric battery.

A battery emits electrical impulses of various kinds, transformable into light, power, heat. The human body is undoubtedly the most powerful dynamo in existence for the carrying on of life. The presiding ego or I AM in each organism determines the particular kind of impulse that the cells shall radiate. The field of dynamic energy is limitless. God is Spirit, and Spirit is the very essence of the ether in which we live, move, and have our being.

God (I AM) will manifest Himself as you make a channel or mold for the manifestation. The little word "as" is very important, for it decides what the manifestation shall be. The Energy flowing through you now is God, but "it" manifests itself "as" you desire. "Whatsoever things ye desire, when ye pray, believe." The flowing iron will not change in Substance, but in form, "as" it passes through the mold. A pipe mold will be used if an iron pipe is desired, a valve mold for a valve, and a wheel mold for a wheel. "As you desire" is the mold which determines the form of manifestation of God.

"Peter denies three times" means that state of consciousness in you, or the disciplined attitude, which will permit only faith in the One Power and the One Presence and is not subject to any other powers. To deny three times is a subjective state of belief which does not allow any argument.

After the creative act and always at dawn the cock crows heralding the birth of the sun (the illumined conscious mind). The dawn appears and the shadows of fear and doubt flee away. Peter denying Jesus (after the flesh) three times, symbolizes the song of triumph, whereby man gives supreme attention to the Lord and Master within . . his own I AM-NESS as Creator and Deliverer from all problems.

When trouble comes do not forget that "I AM the Lord that brought thee out of Egypt." No matter how dense the darkness, how great the tribulations, or how hopeless the bondage, He can bring you out into the promised land of complete emancipation. It is a pleasure to God (I AM) to take us away from our own self-created troubles, the only troubles we shall ever find, for the more we ask of God (I AM) the more we please God (I AM); and He is sufficient, even in the hour of the very greatest need.

He who understands the laws of his mental being, develops his latent powers and uses them intelligently. He does not despise his Passive mental functions, but makes good use of them also, charges them with the duties for which they are best fitted, and is able to obtain wonderful results from their work, having mastered them and trained them to do the bidding of the Higher Self. When they fail to do their work properly he regulates them, and his knowledge prevents him from meddling with them unintelligently, and thereby doing himself harm. He develops the faculties and powers latent within him and learns how to manifest them along the line of Active mentation as well as Passive. He knows that the real man within him is the master to whom both Active and Passive functions are but tools. He has banished Fear, and enjoys Freedom. He has found himself. HE HAS LEARNED THE SECRET OF THE I AM.

The real Individual concealed behind the mask of Personality is YOU . . the Real Self . . the "I" . . that part of you which you are conscious when you say "I AM," which is your assertion of existence and latent power. "Individual" means something that cannot be divided or subtracted from . . something that cannot be injured or hurt by outside forces . . something REAL. And you are an Individual . . a Real Self . . an "I" . . Something endowed with Life, Mind, and Power, to use, as you will.

You can't conceive of a thing that is not part of a state, but the life of any state is in the individual who occupies it. Life cannot be given to a state from without, because God's name is "I AM." It is not "You are" or "They are." God's eternal name is I AM! That is the life of the world. If you would make a state alive, you must be in it. If you are in a lovely, gentle, kind state, you are seeing another as lovely, living graciously, and enjoying life to the utmost. Now, to make that state natural, you must see everyone in your world as lovely, kind, and gentle. Others may not see them in that light, but it doesn't really matter what they think. I am quite sure if I took a survey of what people think of me, no two would agree.

Some would say I am a deceiver, while others I am the nearest thing to God. I would find a range stretching from the devil to God, all based upon the state in which the person is in when called upon to define me. You can be what you want to be if you know and apply this principle, but you are the operant power. It does not operate itself. You may know the law from A to Z, but knowing is not enough. Knowledge must be acted upon. "I AM" is the operant power in you. Put your awareness in the center of your desire. Persist, and your desire will be objectified. Learn to use the law, because there is a long interval between the law and the promise.

Concentration means holding the chosen mental picture to the exclusion of all others till your objective life becomes the picture. "I AM THAT WHICH I THINK MYSELF TO BE!" The Ideal Life is the Real Life and this unseen Ideal Life is the one that alone concerns us. The laws of matter, are the Laws of spirit. They are but reflections of the unseen Laws, because Nature is one. No line can be drawn between the Here and the There; between the present and the past, or the future; between Cause and Effect. The Universe is a Unit, and as such we are to live It. Not to live in it, but to live It, for we are It. This Life of the body that has so troubled us, is the life of appearance, and with appearances hereafter we are not to deal; will deal with eternal verities, i.e. with Ideals which cause these appearances. The goal of every endeavor is Ideal, and that Ideal is REALITY OF SPIRIT. Let this Ideal manifest in perfect faith, by letting it alone, save to hold to it as Will. The Ideal will carry you to the goal of its own manifestation.

When one is absolutely relaxed, conscious only of being conscious, when he has taken his attention away from himself and from his world and fixed his attention only upon the I AM within him, he will be in tune with everything in the Universe and have dominion over it.

How would you conduct yourself if you full realized your oneness with God (I AM), if you could truly believe that He is constantly offering you life, love and every good thing your heart can desire? Well, that is exactly what He is doing! So act as if you already had the thing you want. Visualize it as yours. See the picture clearly in every detail in your mind's eye. Then LET GOD (I AM) make it manifest. Do what you can, of course, with what you have, where you are, but put your dependence upon God (I AM), and LET His good gifts come to you.

The words are these: "I AM from above; you are from below. You are of this world; I AM not of this world. Now I say to you, unless you believe that I AM He you will die in your sins." To sin means to miss the mark, so what he is saying is that unless you believe you already are what you want to be, you will never be it. Would you like to be secure? Then say to yourself and yourself alone: "Unless I believe I AM secure I will die in my sins. I will continue to believe I am insecure; thereby missing my goal in life." Unless you can believe "I AM secure," even though there is not one thing to support it, you will die in your sin and never feel secure, for the name of God is I AM and besides I AM there is no other. Imagination (I AM) is from above. Imagination is not of this world and nothing is impossible to imagine! That is the story of scripture.

There is One Infinite Mind from which all things come; this Mind is through, in and around man; It is the Only Mind that there is, and every time man thinks he uses It. There is One Infinite Spirit, and every time man says, "I AM," he proclaims It. There is One Infinite Substance; and every time man moves, he moves in It. There is One Infinite Law, and every time man thinks he sets It in motion. There is One Infinite God, and every time man speaks to This God, he receives a direct answer. One! One! One! "I AM God and there is none else." There is One Limitless Life which returns to the thinker what he thinks into It. One! One! One! "In all, over all and through all." Talk, live, act, believe and know that you are a center in the One. All the Power there is; all the Presence there is; all the Love there is; all the Peace there is; all the Good there is and the Only God that is, is Omnipresent; consequently, the Infinite is in and through man and is in and through everything. "Act as though I AM and I will Be."

The ancients called the sun the savior of the world as it redeems the world from darkness and death when it ascends the heavens. When John (your intellect) recognizes Jesus, the God-Power within (I AM), you begin to fulfill your desires and aspirations, and your sins (your failure to reach your goal and fulfill your desires) are taken away.

It is in the heart of Being that man says "I AM." It is the I AM of man that is ever one with the Father, as one with God as a drop of water is one with the ocean of which it is a part. Man's being is one with the Being of God and is within itself that which God is. For this reason, man within himself is power, substance and intelligence. It is knowing this that gives him dominion in the realm of form, or makes all form subject to him. "Even the winds and the waves obey him," they said of Jesus, who was the first to claim his God-given right of dominion in earth. Within the heart of man's consciousness lies the creative law through which he expresses his Being. This is the treasure in heaven of which Jesus spoke, and is a treasure because within it lies the power of bringing forth every earthly treasure. It is the cause of things. It is a trinity principle, and through its use "All things are possible," for within it lies the power and substance and intelligence through which all things are created.

You are one with the great "I AM" of the universe. You are part of God. Until you realize that . . and the power it gives you . . you will never know God. God (I AM) has incarnated Himself in man. He seeks expression. Give Him work to do through you, give Him a chance to express Himself in some useful way, and there is nothing beyond your powers to do or to attain.

You have already read in verse five the light shineth in darkness. False concepts, wrong theories, and negative thoughts represent your darkness. If you believe a fan gives you a stiff neck, it is a false light or knowledge and causes suffering in your world. Ideas and concepts which inspire you, thoughts which elevate, dignify, heal, and bless you, represent the Wisdom of God (I AM) which is the true Light. True knowledge of God (I AM) will light up the heaven of your mind and give you peace, serenity, a sense of security, and tranquility. I believe you have a good idea of what the word awareness is all about now. We must remember that we create our own world after the image and likeness of our own mental pictures and thought patterns.

In the midst of conflict, let me become aware of how peaceful my world is, and I will send peace into my world. My authority as I AM has sent peace unto me, for I am conscious of peace. If you know this truth, you will never complain, for you will know you are the cause of your complaint. If you sincerely desire to change your world, however, you must change yourself! If you dislike someone, or think he dislikes you, the cause is not in him and his behavior, but in you. Be honest with yourself and you will discover that whenever you think of him, your conversations are always unpleasant. The new man is incapable of unlovely thoughts or acts. He speaks only kind, loving words.

Mental treatment recognizes that each individual has his identity in mind and is known in Mind by the name he bears. This Subjective Law knows there is a John Smith and a Mary Jones. Why? Because John Smith and Mary Jones know that there is a John Smith and a Mary Jones. But It only knows about them what they know about themselves. Being subjective to their thought, It could not know anything else; consequently, whatever John Smith and Mary Jones say, It says, accepts and does. This is a marvelous concept. Unless we have thought it out, it may seem rather startling. But it means this: that the Law absolutely accepts us at our own valuation. Now this does not mean that it accepts us at an assumption of valuation, but at the actual valuation. It can reflect to us only the actual embodiment of ourselves. It is the deep inner conviction that we carry which decides what is going to happen. So we are each known by the name we bear, and each is daily making some statement about that name. When we say "I AM this or that," we are involving in Mind statements which Mind in turn produces as conditions.

I tell you it is possible to be anything you want to be, for the believer and the God of the universe are one. Don't divorce yourself from God, for he is your I AMness. Believe in your I AMness, for if you do not you will never fulfill your desire. Only by assuming you already are the one you would like to be will you achieve it. It's just as simple as that.

Everything I am telling you is from the Bible. "I kill and I make alive. I wound and I heal and there is none that can deliver out of my hand. I, even I AM He and there is no God besides me. I AM the Lord your God, the holy one of Israel, your Savior and besides me there is no savior." These are the words of God, revealed through his prophets of old. Their prophecy is fulfilled in the New Testament as: "Whatsoever you desire, believe you have received it and you will." That's how easily you apply it, for an assumption, though false and denied by your senses, if persisted in will harden into fact.

Let us turn to the Law, and find what It says, that man is conscious mind or spirit; this stands for his objective faculty. The objective mind of man is his recognition of life in a conscious state; it is the only attribute of man that is volitional, or self-choosing; consequently, it is the spiritual man. The conscious mind of man is the contemplator, the reflector. The Universe is the result of the Contemplation of the Divine Mind, or the Holy Spirit, which is God. God creates by contemplating His own I-AM-NESS; and this contemplation, through law, becomes the objectification of the Self-Realization of the Infinite Mind.

The soul in its incarnation into a form of flesh is like a seed that has been sown in the earth. It must be watered by our thoughts of recognition and quickened by our deep feelings of love for the Creator. It has an affinity only for the truth of the Creator's love; the thoughts and feelings generated by earthly things becloud its faculties and hinder it from receiving its daily sustenance from the I AM within. If the mind of a person is centered wholly upon material things, the soul becomes isolated from the Creator.

If the soul is strong and has had some degree of awakening, it will tire of the dreariness and darkness of mortal vibrations, and when an occasion offers itself by way of sickness or weakness of the body, it will sever its connections with the flesh and return to the freer state of spiritual life, causing death to the body. But it will still be burdened by its personal mind, which it must regenerate. The work of regeneration would have been much easier had the personal mind received and accepted the knowledge of spiritual truths before death, because truth received from the mortal plane of understanding produces a deeper impression on the mind accustomed to dealing with material things.

I tell you, you are all imagination and not a prisoner of anything or anyone, rather you have imprisoned yourself. You have brought all of your experiences into being and you can change them now that you know who you are. When you hear the word Lord, don't think of another. The word is Yod Hey Vav Hey and means I AM, as do the words Father and potter. Your awareness of being is your I AM, your potter who molds your world. To him and him alone lies all of the responsibilities for what is done in your world. Your own wonderful human imagination is the cause of the restrictions on the freedom that you enjoy today.

There is no other cause but the Lord, who is the Father, who is the potter, and if he is your own wonderful human imagination, to whom can you turn to praise or blame for the circumstances of your life? The blind leaders of the blind blame society or the government for the causes of the phenomena of their life. But I tell you, there is no other cause; for there is no one outside of self. Society, the government, your family, or friends, are all within you. Although they appear to be pushed out, there is not a thing that does not now exist in you; as Divine Imagination (the Lord God Almighty) has reproduced Himself in you . . the human imagination; and Divine Imagination contains all things within Himself.

When you affirm "I AM," you speak the name and power of the Divine Being. Your present mind, body and affairs have been generated from limited mortal thoughts and feelings. In a sense, you have taken the name of your Creator in vain when you have affirmed the limited beliefs of mortal thought and feeling. You have said "I AM" mortal, sinful, weak, poor, sick, unsuccessful. According to this limited faith you have created limitations within yourself. Now you can regenerate or reform your mind, body, and affairs from the faith born of the Thought of your Creator. Faith is the substance of things hoped for. Your thought is your faith.

Your faith is only as strong as your thoughts. All the possibilities of a new, strong faith are opened to you as you regenerate your mind by the development of positive thoughts of Truth. Do not separate feeling from thought, for it is the life of thought. You can know the Creator only through your own thought, only as you can conceive of the beauty of Divine Ideas, and express their quality through your own nature. You can know as much of Divine Love and Wisdom as you can generate through your thoughts and feelings. Your capacity will grow forever.

I tell you: everything is possible to the individual when he knows who he is. You are the Joshua of the Old Testament and the Jesus of the New. And Jesus, your own wonderful human imagination, is Jehovah. He is your awareness, but as long as you see Jehovah as someone other than yourself you will not apply this principle. You must be willing to give up all foreign gods, all idols, and return to the one and only God, whose name is in you as your very being! If you were trained in the Christian faith, you were taught to believe that Jesus was on the outside.

But how can you put him to the test if he is another? There never was another Joshua or Jehovah. There is only God, the director of the great dance of life whose dancers are himself.

God plays the part of the bum and dances the dance of poverty. He also plays the part of a millionaire and dances to the tune of millions, as every part is being played by God.

Now, everyone must act from where he is! Ask yourself: where am I? If I AM God, where can I go and God (I AM) is not? If I make my bed in hell, God (I AM) is there. If I make it in heaven, God (I AM) is there, for everything penetrates me! I do not have to physically move. Simply by adjusting my thinking I can move from one state to another.

From beginning to end, the Bible speaks only of the creative power of God (I AM). You can take that same creative power and use it here in the world of Caesar, for it is your own wonderful human imagination. If you will conjure a scene which would imply the fulfillment of your dream and remain faithful to that vision as Paul was to the heavenly vision, your desire will come to pass. Paul did not expect the vision. It came upon him suddenly, like some great catastrophic earthquake. You cannot conjure the vision, it simply happens. But you can conjure a scene which would imply the fulfillment of your desire, remain faithful to it and it will project itself upon the screen of space. I've done it unnumbered times.

Take a simple scene. Would someone congratulate you if they heard of your good fortune? Then allow them to do so. Accept their congratulations, just as you would if they came to you in the flesh. Now remain faithful to that vision. If you need a more complex scene, like two people discussing your success, eavesdrop on them. Listen to their words of praise or envy, then do not forget that vision. Conjured in your imagination, carry it with you, knowing that what it implies will come to pass, for its potency is not in the scene itself, but what the scene implies.

The progress of the individual toward self-mastery is real only to the degree that one brings the negative mind into a higher realization of Consciousness, and causes each particle of one's physical cosmos to evolve and show forth the divine intelligence which has been appropriated and individualized around that person's positive I AM center. Negative or base thoughts and desires fill humanity's nature with a consuming fire, which poisons the blood and burns out the nerve centers. This causes disease and pain in the body, and weakness and discouragement to the mind, hindering the human organism from enjoying the peaceful, vitalizing influx which flows from the soul life. Joy and satisfaction are attributes of the All Mind, and the soul, as an individualized expression of the Over-Soul, contains all the essentials of happiness within itself, and can impart the only true happiness to its human mind and body to the degree that it can gain full and free expression through the positive and negative poles of mind in which it is organized.

God, as your imagination, can never be so far off as even to be near, for the nearness implies separation. Wherever you are, I AM! To say: "I AM" is near, is to claim God is another . . but there is no other. You and God are one, for He is your wonderful human imagination!

Until it is revealed to you, use his name as revealed through his prophet Moses. "And when you go to them just tell them 'I AM' has sent me unto you." Lead them out of the wilderness into light by my name. When you can lead yourself today, no matter where you are, whether you are now bewildered, whether you are unwanted (as you think you are), or unemployed, (as you may be) . . lead yourself from these states of barrenness into states of fruition, a fruitful state, in the name. Just simply assume "I AM", and you name it, hear it, smell it, see it to the best of your ability, and to the degree that you remain loyal to what you are imagining and hearing, you will actually externalize it in your world. Don't judge it before you try it.

When people say Jesus Christ is coming again do not believe them, for Jesus Christ has never left you. Did he not say: "Lo, I AM with you always, even to the end of the age?" Then how can you look for him to return? Scripture states that Christ was taken up into the kingdom of heaven (which is within) and that he will come in the same manner as he was taken up. If Christ (God's creative power) is in you, he cannot come from without. Although he seems to be invisible, Christ has never left you, as you cannot detach yourself from imagination.

You have the capacity to believe. You may believe in something stupid, but you believe and your belief will make it work. The one I speak of as God (I AM) is your mightier self, yet your slave, for purposes of his own. He waits on you as indifferently and as swiftly when your will is evil as when it is good. He does it by conjuring images of good and evil just as though they were real. Allowing you to imagine whatever you desire, he projects it upon this screen of space in order for you to experience it. You can move into it so naturally and so easily you can forget the thoughtless moment when the seed was planted, and therefore do not recognize your own harvest.

I ask you to use this power called the law. Simply determine what you want and imagine a scene which would imply you have realized it. Enter into the spirit of the scene. Participate in it by giving it sensory vividness. Then relax as you feel its reality. Don't consider the means. Know your desire is already an accomplished fact and you are now reveling in it. Then have faith, for faith is loyalty to your unseen reality. Your imaginal act, although unseen, is reality for God did it. If I asked you who is imagining it, you would respond: "I AM" and that is God's name forever and forever.

As we are told, "Do you not realize that Jesus Christ (I AM) is in you?" Then test yourselves to see if you really realize it. Put yourself to the test If I say, "Jesus Christ," and your mind jumps on the outside to something other than yourself, you have failed the test, for you are told: "Do you not realize that Jesus Christ is in you? . . unless, of course," said he, "you fail to meet the test!" Well, you have just had the test. So, when I use the words, "Jesus Christ," and something on the outside comes to you, you have failed the test!, for Jesus Christ (I AM) is in you. If I go to Him in my prayer, where would I go but to myself? He became as I AM, that I may be as He is. He actually became me. He is in me as my own wonderful human imagination, for "by Him all things were made, and without Him was not anything made that was made," so I go within and appropriate the state.

So, I only ask you to be as faithful to any imaginal state in this world, no matter what it is. In everyone God resides. Everyone has to say, "I AM." That is God. I AM Einstein, I AM Neville. I AM is God. Neville is a tiny thing resting on the foundation that is God. I AM rich . . that is a tiny thing on the foundation of God, and God is Infinity, God is Everything. Therefore, whatever you say, before you say it, you say, "I AM".

The first great discovery that man made was that he could think. This was the day when he rose from the ground and said, "I AM." This marked the first great day of personal attainment; and from that day man became an individual and had to make all further progress himself; any compulsory evolution stopped when man became an individual, and from that day he had to work in conscious union with Nature and Her forces; but he did not have to work alone, for Instinctive Life has always been with him and will never depart from him. Instinctive Life desires that man shall express more, and yet more, of its own limitless possibilities. Man is evolving from an Infinite basis; behind him is the great Unknown but not the great unknowable; for the unknown becomes known through man, and whatever more Instinctive Life is to do for him must be done through him. Nature must work through man in order to work for him. This is true all along the line of life and endeavor.

To say:"I AM going to be rich," will not make it happen; you must believe riches in by claiming within yourself: "I AM rich." You must believe in the present tense, because the active, creative power that you are, is God (I AM). He is your awareness, and God (I AM) alone acts and is. His name forever and ever is "I AM" therefore, he can't say: "I will be rich" or "I was rich" but "I AM rich!"

Begin now to actively, constantly, use your imagination; for as you prove its creative power on this level, you are awakening to a higher level and birth into the spirit world where you know yourself to be God. Prove to yourself that you are God by feeling your desire is now an accomplished fact. Listen to your friends talk about you. Are they rejoicing because of your good fortune, or are they expressing envy? Imagine their words are true. Persist in imagining they are true. Continue to imagine your desire is already an accomplished fact; and when it is objectively realized, proof will be yours.

Think of something lovely you would like to give another. Then ask yourself if you gave it to him and he wouldn't accept it, would you want to keep it for yourself? If, for instance, you gave a friend a million dollars and he would not accept it, would you be willing to keep it? I'm sure you would. Then imagine giving the money to him, then give to others in the same way. You may not even have a bank account; but you can still give, because there is no one to give to but yourself! There is only God whose name is I AM!

Reality is controlled by feeling, as told us in the 27th chapter of Genesis. The central character in this chapter is the state called Isaac, who has two sons . . Esau and Jacob. Esau is clothed in objective reality, while Jacob wears subjective reality as longings, wishes, and desires. When Jacob disguised himself as an objective fact, Isaac said: "Come near that I may feel you to determine whether you are Esau or not." And when he asked: "Are you really Esau?" Jacob answered, "I AM."

Put yourself into a subjective state. Then feel the objectivity of the state by giving it sensory vividness and tones of reality.

Then deceive yourself into believing that the image into which you have entered is now objectively real. Do that, and you have entered the state called Isaac. And we are told that when Isaac once more saw his objective world, Esau returned and Jacob disappeared. Then he realized that he had been self-deceived, but could not take back the blessing given to the subjective state. Although your objective world denies the reality of what you have done in your imagination, that which you have subjectively assumed is on its way to supplant your objective world and become your Esau.

Man is created and left to discover himself, and on the road to this self-discovery he experiences the creations of his own imaginations which ultimately show him the Truth and lead to real freedom. There is an interesting myth in regard to the creating of man which may serve to point out this fact.

It is said that when the gods decided to make man, and make him a Divine Being, they held a long discussion as to where would be the best place to hide his Divinity. Some of the gods suggested that it be hidden in the earth, but others argued that someday man would penetrate the earth and so discover himself; it was then suggested that it be hidden in the depths of the sea, but this idea was rejected, for man would go under the sea and there discover his true nature; it was next suggested that his real nature should be deposited somewhere in the air, but this also was rejected, for he would surely fly through the air and find himself. After a long discussion it was finally agreed that the best place to hide man's Divinity would be IN THE INNERMOST NATURE OF MAN HIMSELF . . this being the last place he would look to find it! This discovery would not be made until he had had all the experience necessary to complete a well-rounded life. "The Word is very nigh unto thee, in thy mouth, and in thy heart, that thou mayest do it." Of course, this is a fable, but how clearly it sets forth the reality of the case! The word is really in our own mouths, and every time we say "I AM" we are repeating it; for "I AM" is the secret of nature and the emblem of Eternity.

The laws of matter are responsive to the superior laws of mind, and "miracles", so-called, do not set aside natural laws but merely show that natural laws are subservient to the superior forces of the Universal Mind. There are no miracles in the sense of the violation of natural laws.

"All things are possible" to the human mind when it learns to exercise and direct the powers of the soul as did the prophets and the mystics of the ages. Then natural laws prove obedient to the superior law, of which they are but effects.

We can overcome many of the limitations of the material body by developing in our flesh a more positive degree of vitality. Affirm again and again: I AM VITALITY. Think vitality, breathe vitality, eat vitality, and know that you are the unlimited vitality of the Creator: thus, you will become a magnet for Almighty Vitality. Think toward each organ of your body: YOU ARE VITALITY. You are so filled and thrilled with vitality that there is no place for disease or decay in you. ALL IS VITALITY. Keep this up unceasingly and it will make you so positively vital that health and happiness will reign throughout your whole being.

We have all wondered why we do not understand more truth than we do or why it is necessary to understand at all, since God is all-wise and all-present. Understanding is one of the essential parts of your I AM identity. Man is a focal point in God consciousness and expresses God. Therefore he must understand the processes that bring about that expression. Infinite Mind is here with all its ideas as a resource for man, and what we are or become is the result of our efforts to accumulate in our own consciousness all the attributes of infinite Mind. We have learned that we can accumulate ideas of power, strength, life, love, and plenty. How should we use these ideas or bring them into outer expression without understanding? Where shall we get this understanding save from the source of all ideas, the one Mind? "But if any of you lacketh wisdom, let him ask of God, who giveth to all liberally and upbraideth not; and it shall be given him."

Giving our attention to anything negative is idolatry or the worship of false gods. In prayer we must separate our thoughts and give our attention to God (I AM) and His Omnipotence and give power to nothing else. To give power to conditions, circumstances, and external causes is to practice idolatry. We must use disciplined imagination or our capacity to imagine the end and feel its reality and our prayer will be answered.

All things are what I AM. Creation, ideas, things, forms . . are not separate from Me, rather they are "Me" . . embodied. I create, form, bring into existence, give body to . . the ideas that are ever-present in the Mind I AM. Creation is brought into expressed images from the Source or Origin I AM. All "things/forms . . the embodiment of ideas" are brought forth into visible expression because this is what the Omni-active does. This is the activity of the Omnipresent, Omnipotent and Omniscient One I AM.

Now, in order to prove that the law works, you must try it. Have a goal. Your goal may be peace of mind, health or marriage. You name it. Knowing your own wonderful human imagination is the one and only cause of your life, conceive a scene which, if true, would imply the fulfillment of your goal. Do not allow yourself to observe the action, but put yourself in the center of the scene and allow your friends to congratulate you on your good fortune. Accept their congratulations without embarrassment. Enter into the spirit of the scene and remain there until it feels real, then drop it in confidence that the imaginal act was performed by God. How do I know this? Because God's name forever and ever is I AM.

Here is the "outer man" called Neville who came into the world first. This is the "Esau" of Scripture. And then after that, comes another one, . . my own wonderful human imagination; and that's the "Jacob." This is the "twin" that comes into the world. They aren't two separate little boys. This is the story; this is an adumbration of that which comes later into the New Testament; that the one who could say, "I AM from above and you are from below; you are of this world; I am not of this world." So the Being that is speaking is your own wonderful human imagination that in Scripture is called "Jesus Christ."

And the "thing below" is the body that you are "wearing," and that is "of this world." You see, we are dealing with the most fantastic mystery in the world, the mystery of imagining. That's what Fawcett said: "The secret of imagining is the greatest of all problems, to the solution of which every man should aspire, for supreme power, supreme wisdom, supreme delight lie in the far-off solution of this mystery," . . because you are actually solving the problem of God. If you can solve the problem of imagining, you are solving the problem of God!

Among the seven sacred names given to Jehovah by the Hebrew priesthood is "Jehovah-shammah," meaning "Jehovah is there." Jehovah is the name of the ever-living I AM. When the mystic desired to commune with the omnipresent life he did not speak the name aloud but silently intoned, "Jehovah-shammah!" This pervasion of his I AM with the ever-living I AM harmonized the spiritual man with his source, and the individual was merged with the universal. A certain mystery has always accompanied the use of the sacred name, and the priesthood gained their ascendancy over the people by performing marvelous works through the silent and audible intoning of words charged with thoughts of spiritual power.

I urge you to shape your world from within and no longer from without. Describe yourself as you would like to be seen by others and believe your words. Walk in the assumption they are true and . . because no power can thwart God . . what He is imagining, you will experience. You are not someone apart from God, for I AM cannot be divided. The Lord, our God, is one I AM, not two! If God's I AM and your I AM is the same I AM, define what you would like to be. Then believe you are the Lord! Be like the lady who transformed a streetcar into a cruise. Lose yourself in your new state, while your world on the outside remains, momentarily, the same.

From this platform I teach that I and my Father are one. Being one, my Father can never be so far off as even to be near, for nearness implies separation. What is there in you that can't even be near? Imagination! You cannot separate yourself from imagination. You can't claim: "I AM" and point to it as something on the outside. It is impossible to separate yourself from the sense of being, so in the sense of I AMness, you are imagining. If this sense of oneness is your Father, do you really believe in him? If so, to what extent does your confession in words conform to your deep, deep conviction?

The Ever-Present Great Spirit is waiting to give you all the power that you can use. The Creator's love desires to satisfy the hunger of your immortal nature. The I AM has already given you eternal life, but that does not necessarily mean that you have awakened to that fact. The Infinite Presence will aid you to outgrow all your physical and spiritual limitations to the degree that you fulfill the laws of your being and exert your own will to demand your rightful inheritance as a son or daughter of the Creator while making wise use of the powers that you receive. Spiritual science shows you the way.

Seeing that All is Mind, All is Good, All is the Creator, the enlightened man and woman are one with the Creator and all Divine expressions; there is no limitation to their vision or to their knowledge, for they are divine in every faculty. They can hear all the vibratory whisperings of the Good in all the universe, and enjoy the blending of their minds with the Mind that fills infinity, thus partaking of divine Omniscience. Realizing that they are all Spirit, and that there is no law but the Will of the Creator, and that they themselves are that Will, whatever they will must be effected through their nature.

They can become positive to the vibrations of light so that mortal eyes cannot see their form, and they can make themselves so positive to the attraction of earth that water will seem a solid substance to their feet. The enlightened man and woman can exert a powerful and beneficial sway over other natures who are willing to be influenced by their positive will of goodness and peace, which quickens them with the vitality of Eternity and satisfies their spiritual natures with the living Bread of Life. Glory to the perfected man and woman, for they are the personality of the Creator, the I AM.

The proposition that the seemingly insignificant individual I AM contains infinite creative capacity appears absurd to the thoughtless, but we have numerous examples of extraordinary capacity for expansion in the little seeds that bring forth gigantic trees. The Scriptures plainly teach that men may become gods. Adam was expelled from the Garden of Eden because Jehovah realized that he might appropriate eternal life and live forever in his ignorance. When man realizes that "death and life are in the power of the tongue" and begins to use his "I AM" statements wisely, he has the key that unlocks the secret chambers of existence in heaven and earth.

There is nothing God cannot do! Do not think that one who is fabulously rich has an influx of spirit which differs from yours. He is imagining wealth, either wittingly or unwittingly; but you can do it knowingly. If he does not know what he is doing, he can lose his wealth and not know how to recover it. I am asking you, regardless of your financial situation, to assume wealth, knowingly. If, tomorrow you would again return to your former state, bring wealth back by claiming "I AM wealthy," for there is only one God. He who creates poverty also creates wealth, as there is no other creator.

The God who is love cannot hear the prayer of the man who is not love. Love and cooperation will yet be found to be the greatest business principle on earth. "God is Love." We will make our unity with all people, with all life. We will affirm that God in us is unified with God in all. This One is now drawing into our life all love and fellowship. I AM one with all people, with all things, with all life. As I listen in the silence the voice of all humanity speaks to me and answers the love that I hold out to it.

This great love that I now feel for the world is the love of God, and it is felt by all and returned from all. Nothing comes in between because there is nothing but love to come in between. I understand all people and that understanding is reflected back to me from all people. I help, therefore I AM helped. I uplift, therefore I AM uplifted. Nothing can mar this perfect picture of myself and my relations with the world; it is the truth, the whole truth, and nothing but the truth. I AM now surrounded by all love, all friendship, all companionship, all health, all happiness, all success. I AM one with life. I wait in the silence while the Great Spirit bears this message to the whole world.

To be born again means to think in a new way, to undergo an internal transformation of the mind by realizing and knowing that God (I AM) is the Spiritual Power within, which can be contacted through man's thought, thereby bringing about the rebirth of consciousness. Nicodemus judged by the visible state. When we are born again, we judge by the invisible state. Everything in the Bible is intended to convey a special meaning, and the main point is to know what is meant. We are not at all concerned whether such a conversation actually took place between two men two thousand years ago or not. We are primarily interested in what it means to us, and how we can use the drama to rise in the knowledge of God (I AM).

As we center in the formless presence of God and become responsive only to that which is Good, two things will happen. We shall know sensations never before experienced and shall emerge with definite guidance or leading. In praying, we talk to God and his answer comes in the form of inspiration. The voice of Intuition that speaks in the Silence is the infallible Word of God. The intuitive faculty is by far the most valuable and yet the most delicate instrument of Mind. It is the guiding force of the Soul. But unless we search for it with great patience and are obedient to its slightest prompting, we shall miss it. It is the still small voice of the I AM.

I wanted a trip I could not afford, yet I traveled over 5,000 miles by being still and saying to myself: "My awareness (I AM) is God and all things are possible to him. therefore what I am imagining will come to pass." Then I began to imagine I was on a ship sailing towards Barbados. I remained faithful to that act, when suddenly . . after twelve years . . I received a letter from the family saying they would take care of all of my expenses if I would come home for Christmas. So I proved it. Then I tried it again and again, and the more I tried it the more I realized that the statement in the 46th Psalm was true: that God really is my own wonderful consciousness, for I learned to be still and know that I AM God.

The highest mental practice is to listen to this Inner Voice and to declare for Its Presence. The greater a man's consciousness of this Indwelling I AM is, the more power he will have. This will never lead to illusion but will always lead to Reality. All great souls have known this and have constantly striven to let the Mind of God come out through their mentalities. "The Father that dwelleth in Me, He doeth the works." This was the declaration of the great Master, and it should be ours also; not a limited sense of life but a limitless one.

Here is a vivid experience of a duplicate dream, and scripture tells us that if the dream repeats itself the thing is fixed, and the Lord will shortly bring it to pass. God's creative power is now unfolding in my friend. Now he knows his own wonderful human imagination is God. That the great I AMness in man is God and that all things are possible to Him. Now the challenge is his. Whatever he wants is! All he has to do is adjust his thinking to the state desired until it becomes alive within him, and at that moment the state will objectify itself in his world.

Marvelous are the beauties of divine thought. Our thoughts shall be pure and exalted, free from that mortal bondage, that physical limitation that characterizes the thoughts of men. The attractions of the external world are not strong enough to keep our thoughts from soaring to the Father. We shall deny the lesser attractions and responded wholly to the supreme attraction of Divine Love. The I AM Power is the omnipotent One and brings sweet rest and peace to all who live close to it and obey its voice of wisdom. Strive to open your eyes to the beauty of your own soul, the I, the inward Spirit that can heal and save if you recognize it as God in you and live up to its idea.

"I AM come that ye might have life and have it more abundantly." The abundance that we express is always commensurate with our recognition of the Law (I AM). The greatest good that can come to man is the realization of the full and complete Spirit of Good within himself. All seeking must be based on the fundamental principle that God is Wholeness and Completion; that He is Mind, Intelligence and Life; that as a man thinketh in his heart (Soul, Mind), so is he. The creative medium of God is His thought. Freedom and bondage are both in the Law of Mind. Negative thinking produces bondage. Positive thinking produces freedom. Negative thinking is thought not consistent with the essential goodness and wholeness of God.

Learn to live in your imagination (I AM) morning, noon, and night. This gentleman whose experiences I shared with you tonight told me that when he first heard me he thought I was crazy; but he tried it, and although it didn't make sense it worked. I know the law and the promise do not make sense from a worldly point of view, yet I tell you: there is a plan of redemption buried in you which will erupt in the fullness of time and you will experience all that is said of a man called Jesus in scripture. Then you will know he was never a physical being, but the name of a plan. Jesus is Jehovah, who is your own wonderful I AM.

Every time you send out a thought of wholehearted faith in the I AM part of yourself, you set in motion a chain of causes that must bring the results you seek. Ask whatsoever you will in the name of the Christ, the I AM, the divine within, and your demands will be fulfilled; both heaven and earth will hasten to do your bidding. But when you have asked for something, be on the alert to receive it when it comes. People complain that their prayers are not answered when, if we knew the truth, they are not awake to receive the answer when it comes. If you ask for money, do not look for an angel from the skies to bring it on a golden platter, but keep your eyes open for some fresh opportunity to make money, an opportunity that will come as sure as you live.

Although the churches teach that another, greater than yourself, said: "Unless you believe that I AM He, you will die in your sins" . . these words were spoken by the human imagination! And because imagination is one, and you can't get away from that oneness, don't think of another. Accept these words in the first person, present tense; for unless you believe that you already are what you want to be, you will die in your sins by leaving your desire unfulfilled. If you do not believe you are all imagination, you will continue in your former belief, worshipping a God on the outside and not within.

I ask you to believe me, for "Unless you believe that I AM He you will die in your sins." You will miss the mark and never reach your goal unless you believe that you are right now the man you want to be. Is happiness your goal? Then assume it, for unless you assume "I AM happy," you will remain unhappy. You want to be secure? Then assume "I AM secure." That is the only way you will attain it. I AM Imagination, the only power in the world, for Imagination is God. Unless I imagine I AM the man I want to be, I will continue to imagine I am the man I do not want to be. No power on the outside can make me other than what I think I AM. I must assume my own divinity, and as I do it will unfold within me.

All the poetry, wit, knowledge and art of the ages cannot alter the fact that love alone begets love, peace alone attracts peace, only that which goes forth in joy can return with gladness . . give and to you shall be given, and the type multiplied, good measure, running over and pressed down. You need not force or coerce, but you must obey the law. If you can see God in everything, then God will look back at you through everything. This is the meaning of that saying: "Act as though I AM, and I will be." This is the law of give and take. When the time comes that nothing goes forth from you other than that which you would be glad to have return, then you will have reached your heaven.

We have learned that the discovery of God has to be linked up inevitably with Self discovery, that the Universe in which we live is spiritual and not material, that there is only One Mind, to which time and space are nothing, and that this Mind of God is really our Mind. We learned, too, that there is one Substance . . the Substance of our own mind . . which is always active in the soul and ready to take form on the surface. Since the whole process through which the I AM works is one of consciousness, one must look to consciousness for everything needful in his life. Man is solely dependent upon himself . . upon his own consciousness and the power of his own Mind. He becomes masterful to the degree that he is able to harmonize his consciousness with his own divine Mind and to recognize that Mind is the Substance of all things. Mind does not become things; It is things.

We have a right to choose what we shall induce in Mind. The way that our thoughts are to become manifested we cannot always see; but we should not be disturbed if we do not see the way, because effect is potential in cause; "I AM Alpha and Omega." and all that comes between cause and effect. Cause and effect are really One, and if we have a given cause set in motion the effect will have to equal this cause. One is the inside and the other the outside of a concept or idea.

In the Book of John, he tells an incredible story, saying: "I AM God the Father. When you see me, you see the Father. Do you not know that I AM in the Father and the Father in me?" Making one fantastic statement after the other, he adds: "I have told you before it takes place, so that when it does take place you will believe that I AM He." For we are told: "Unless you believe that I AM He, you die in your sins." John emphasizes over and over again that you must believe you are the one you would like to be, or you will never become it. Rather, you will remain what you believe yourself to be right now. Your belief is always externalizing itself on the screen of space. It has to, for it is in you and not out there. When your belief becomes a fact and appears solidly real on the outside, it is because it is supported by you on the inside. The day you cease to believe in it, it will fade, for everything must be built on the foundation of belief. I believe I AM a success. I will remain a success only to the extent that I continue to believe I AM.

Since you are one with the Father, you say not, "I need bread," but "I AM bread, I AM supply. I have supply of which you know not." If God (I AM) is infinite, if God (I AM) is your being, then your very being contains everything you will ever need from now unto eternity. All you need to do is not to try to acquire or attain, but to let what is already embodied within you appear outwardly as form.

Now here is the story. He said, "Except you be born again, you cannot enter the kingdom of heaven." The wise man said, "How is it possible a man my age may once again enter my mother's womb and be born again?" He said, "You, a master of Israel and you do not know? Except you be born of water and the spirit, ye can in no wise enter the kingdom of heaven." Then he gives this clue, "As Moses lifted up the serpent in the wilderness, even so must the son of man be lifted up." ...As Moses lifted up the serpent... do you think a man lifted up a brazen serpent as told in the story and that everyone who looked on it was instantly healed and those who would not look were not cured? It's not any serpent. A serpent is a symbol of the power of endless self-reproduction. For the serpent sheds its skin, and yet does not die. Man must be like the serpent, who grows and outgrows. So I must now learn the art of dying that I may live, rather than, I would say killing that I may survive. I die, by laying down all that I now believe, and I lift myself up to the belief that I AM what I want to be. That's how I do it.

The affirmation, "I AM whole, perfect, strong, powerful, loving, harmonious and happy", will bring about harmonious conditions. The reason for this is because the affirmation is in strict accordance with the Truth, and when truth appears every form of error or discord must necessarily disappear.

Believe me. Make imagination your one solid foundation.
Do this and you will enjoy a freedom you have not known before. It is a fantastic freedom! Just imagine and it's done! Imagination is the only foundation. No other foundation can anyone lay than that which is laid, which is Jesus Christ. Man has tried to lay other foundations in the many isms of the world. These are not Jesus Christ, for he is man's I AMness, man's human imagination, and there is no other God. Hear, O Israel, the Lord our God, the Lord is one, whose name forever and ever is I AM! Accept awareness as your way of life, and you will find a freedom you have never known before. You will become aware of the fact that everyone and everything is yourself pushed out. You will awaken as God, the father of all life, to realize that although things appear to die they do not, for nothing dies in (imagination) Christ.

All things exist as a potentiality, as a possibility, now. "I AM Alpha and Omega." Try to get a recognition of your desire and pass the whole thing over to Mind, and let It operate. Just know that the desire is already a fact, and quietly say to yourself, as often as the thought comes into mind: "It is done." The lighter the thought is, the less care or worry over it, the better. The best work is done when the element of struggle is entirely left out.

I firmly believe that this principle which we profess, is the Savior that was to come. That it is the Principle which is to redeem the world from all present ills. It is as real a Principle as is the recognition of one and one are two, the real basis of that calculation that weighs stars and measures the path of comets. We have the perception of Truth; Truth has no limit; knows neither time nor space. I AM truth! It may take millions of years for the majority of the race to perceive this, but what of it? Millions of years ago some primeval ancestor saw possibilities for himself that none other saw. He expressed.

His expression has become the instinct of the race. So this perception of immortality, however crudely expressed now as belief of an immortality in the flesh, but which is truly immortality outgrown the flesh, will sometime be the instinct of the race. The one Affirmation that will usher in that "Promised day," which comes, not to numbers, but to the individuals is . . I AM SPIRIT! To this realization this crusade of New Thought leads us. Under its inspiration, Man frees himself from the last remnant of the animal and awakens to the recognition of himself as Spirit.

If, in the early history of the planet, atoms had not begun to be organized by that Intelligent Presence to build forms, the human form could never have been produced. The human body is the most perfect corporeal organization that has yet been evolved in nature by the progressive power of the I AM. This demonstration of Organization is not limited to the material world. It is the formative power of the spiritual worlds as well.

We see an intelligent power working to organize atoms into forms for the expression of various qualities, and we see the same power working through human intelligence to draw together minds of like motive and thought for the fulfillment of ideals. What we see "nature" doing seemingly in a blind way, and what we see human beings doing however imperfectly, we may be sure that more spiritualized "nature" and more spiritual beings are doing in harmony with a greater degree of wisdom and a freer expression of power that pertains to higher states of being.

May I tell you: you have the power within to create anything! Let people be what they want to be, while you set goals for yourself. It doesn't matter what has happened in your life or what the evidence of your senses tells you, the power of the universe is in you. That power is the Lord Christ Jesus, whose name is I AM. You will never know it however unless you test him, for only then will you realize that Jesus Christ is in you. I was taught Christ was on the outside somewhere in space. But I took the challenge and tested myself, to discover that I AM creative.

He that losses his life shall find it in the Universal Source. The only thing that can be lost (set aside) are the false belief of the limited personal self. Divine Substance and Power cannot function in a divided or personal consciousness. The mind must be One and the attitude impersonal before we can experience the Power. Greater is he that is in you than he that is in the world. The Impersonal Life is the I AM or spiritual consciousness, which says, If any man will come after me, let him deny himself and take up his cross daily. The cross represents the Universal Mind of God through which the false beliefs of personal consciousness are denied or set aside by the God Consciousness. By lifting one's thought to the Universal Mind, one crosses out all that is opposed to or at variance with God.

Every man who lives might be considered as a branch of the Tree of Life, I AM is the tree. All men live, move, and have their being in it. The seven billion people that walk the earth are branches of God. They do not, however, bring forth fruit (harmony, peace, and joy) unless they are rooted in the Vine.

The sap (inspiration, guidance, and power) is then able to come to them from God within. Without this knowledge, man accomplishes nothing. His sense of isolation, separating him from the One Power, continues. The Inner Voice is constantly urging man to go forward to do, to be, and to have. Man listens to the verdict and announcement of his senses which condemn him to the prison of fear, worry, or impotency. The outer world says, "You can't." The inner world says, "You can." Who is going to win? You determine that. If you listen to the voice of failure, it will criticize, condemn, and accuse you. You will sink into despondency and remorse.

We are all actually one. So, if I stand here now and lose myself in an imaginal act, I AM influencing the entire world . . influencing every one who can be used to aid me in the objectification what am imagining. So, do it lovingly. Whatever you do, do lovingly, . . I don't care what it is. And if you are ever in doubt, do the loving thing, which is called by the simple, simple term the "Golden Rule'. "Do unto others as you would have them do unto you." So, if you are ever in doubt, use that as your rule, and you can't go wrong.

We must lift up this serpent of sense, as Moses lifted up the serpent in the wilderness, and control it in the name of Christ. Eliminate all negative thoughts that come into your mind. Yet do not spend all your time in denials but give much of it to the clear realization of the everywhere present and waiting substance and life. Some of us have in a measure inherited "hard times" by entertaining the race thought so prevalent around us. Do not allow yourself to do this. Remember your identity, that you are a son of God and that your inheritance is from Him. You are the heir to all that the Father has. Let the I AM save you from every negative thought. The arrows that fly by day and the pestilence that threatens are these negative race thoughts in the mental atmosphere. The I AM consciousness, your Savior, will lead you out of the desert of negation and into the Promised Land of plenty that flows with milk and honey.

You need not be concerned about how this will be accomplished. Your imagination will use whatever natural means are necessary to bring it about. "I AM the beginning and the end." "My ways are past finding out." What you do in imagination is an instantaneous creative act. However, in this three-dimensional world, events appear in a time sequence. Make your inner conversations conform to your imaginal act. You have planted a seed and you will soon see the harvest of that which you have sowed.

Many times I have heard someone say: "I believe that imagining creates reality, but I once imagined something and it never came to pass." Then I ask: "What are you doing, saying: 'I once imagined it' and not imagining it now?' For God's name is I AM, not I did!" Always thinking of God as someone outside of himself, man finds it difficult to keep the tense, but God is the human imagination and there is no other God. When you imagine you may include others, but do not think in terms of influence. Rather, think only in terms of clarity of form.

Perhaps a friend would like a better job, more money, and greater responsibility. Before you imagine, take a moment and clarify the form your imaginal act will take. Are you giving the celebration party or is he? Who will be there? Fill the room with those who would want to share in the celebration. Raise your glass and say: "Here's to your fabulous new job, your salary increase, and the challenge of your greater responsibility!" Don't think in terms of trying to influence the friend's boss, for he could die or be discharged. Just go to the end. Toast the event, and do not think of influencing others.

Are you willing to become enamored over a desire that much? Are you willing to fall in love with its fulfillment that you imagine it is yours now? If so, I promise you it will out picture itself in your world. And when it does, you will have found Christ, for the words of scripture: "By him all things are made and without him is not anything made that is made," are false. When you test your imagination you will find He who produced your desire and the Maker of all things! I have tested him numberless times. I have taught this principle to others who have tested him and shared their experiences with me. Now I know who Jesus Christ really is.

The words, "Unless you believe that I AM He, you will die in your sins," are not spoken on the outside, but on the inside. Now wearing a garment of flesh, my words appear to be coming from without, and one day I will seem to die and become a historical fact. But I am not speaking as an outer man. I am speaking as the true Jesus Christ, who comes in every individual by unfolding his story as recorded in scripture. There is only one story, and only one being to play the part. That being is God (I AM). It is he alone who acts and is in all things.

If I gave a Stradivarius to one who had mastered the violin he could lift me to the nth degree of joy, but if I put the same violin in the hands of one who could not play it, he would shortly drive me insane. It's the same violin, yet one brings harmony while the other brings discord. You kill and make alive out of the same instrument, which is your own wonderful human imagination. You may make many discords until you learn how to play. We are here in this world of educated darkness learning to play the instrument which is God (I AM). You may not know anyone who would give you $10,000 right now, but if you believe all things are possible to God (I AM) and you know that God (I AM) is your human imagination, you can imagine you have the money, persist in your belief and you will have it. How, I do not know; I only know that according to your belief will it be done unto you.

It is well to read a few words of faith in order to lift your mind above disturbing details and affairs into the exalted State of Mind in which the words were written. Affirm silently, and when possible sing or intone audibly, the Sacred Name of your Being: I AM. This simple practice will make you more vibrant with conscious, forceful faith, and you will realize greater power as an organizer of your home life and affairs.

Within everyone's brain, there is an area where The I AM dwells. When this divine I AM within awakes, it vibrates to the same state of Will, Thought, and Feeling as the organized Angel Hosts. As States of Mind are finer and different from conditions of matter, so this exalted State is finer and different from the States of Mind which constitute the spiritual worlds related to humanity's mental and moral nature.

Deeper and finer and more hidden within their minds than any of their present experience of thought and feeling is this supra-conscious I AM. The dark spiritual world of selfish spirits vibrates to a like selfish quality of will, thought and feeling in the conscious and subconscious mind of the human brain. The Angel Hosts radiate rays of light to the I AM in every soul in the physical and spiritual world. The Light was in the world, in the brain of humanity, but the human mind was so darkened by materiality and selfishness that the Light was not apprehended or used to clear the mind and make it a Place of Light and Love.

Man must have avenues through which to express himself. These avenues are the "help meet" designed by Jehovah God. Man represents wisdom. It is not good for wisdom to act alone; it must be joined with love if harmony is to be brought forth. Both the soul and the body are helpmeets to man (spirit), avenues through which he expresses the ideas of Mind. It is on the soul or substance side of consciousness that ideas are "identified," that is, "named." Whatever we recognize a thing to be, that it becomes to us because of the naming power vested in man (wisdom). "Every beast of the field" and the "cattle" represent ideas of strength, power, vitality, and life.

These ideas must be recognized by the I AM before they can be formed. "The birds of the heavens" represent free thoughts and the interchange between the subconscious and the conscious activities of mind. Man has power to name all ideas that are presented to his conscious mind, whether they come from within or without. Wisdom, the masculine phase of man, needs a helpmeet or balance. Love in the soul (woman) has not yet been developed and established in substance.

I AM Using My Will Power

Say these words several times earnestly and positively, immediately after finishing this article. Then repeat them frequently during the day, at least once an hour, and particularly when you meet something that calls for the exercise of Will Power. Also repeat them several times after you retire and settle yourself for sleep. Now, there is nothing in the words unless you back them up with the thought. In fact, the thought is "the whole thing," and the words only pegs upon which to hang the thought. So think of what you are saying, and mean what you say. You must use Faith at the start, and use the words with a confident expectation of the result. Hold the steady thought that you are drawing on your storehouse of Will Power, and before long you will find that thought is taking form in action, and that your Will Power is manifesting itself. You will feel an influx of strength with each repetition of the words. You will find yourself overcoming difficulties and bad habits, and will be surprised at how things are being smoothed out for you.

"**I AM the light of the world.**" I AM, the knowledge that I exist, is a light by means of which what passes in my mind is rendered visible. Memory, or my ability to mentally see what is objectively present, proves that my mind is a mirror, so sensitive a mirror that it can reflect a thought.

I AM Asserting the Mastery of My Real Self

Repeat these words earnestly and positively during the day at least once an hour, and particularly when you are confronted with conditions which tempt you to act on the lines of the lesser self instead of following the course dictated by the Real Self. In the moment of doubt and hesitation say these words earnestly, and your way will be made clear to you. Repeat them several times after you retire and settle yourself to sleep. But be sure to back up the words with the thought inspiring them, and do not merely repeat them parrot-like.

Form the mental image of the Real Self asserting its mastery over the lower planes of your mind . . see the King on his Throne. You will become conscious of an influx of new thought, and things which have seemed hard for you will suddenly become much easier. You will feel that you have yourself well in hand, and that YOU are the master and not the slave. The thought you are holding will manifest itself in action, and you will steadily grow to become that which you have in mind.

When you dream tonight of numberless people and awaken in the morning to find them gone, where did they go? Are they not all in you, created by and acted by you? Then are you not protean? You, all Imagination, are God (I AM) the dreamer, imagining the many parts you are playing. This very moment is a part of your dream, and those around you are there, playing their parts because you are imagining them. You are playing the part of your husband, your wife, your children, your friends, and your enemies. They are all you, for there is nothing but God (I AM) (Imagination).

Our senses are really God's senses; when we realize this, we cannot have poor eyesight, poor hearing, poor health or poor anything. I AM sees through our eyes, hears through our ears, thinks through our minds, works through our bodies. He is All-in-All. I AM declares health and power in every corpuscle, every vein, every cell, every nerve and every atom of the body saying unto them, Be ye therefore perfect even as your Father in heaven is perfect. I AM will fill the body to overflowing with Divine power and health, for I AM is within every cell, and every cell is alive with the Universal Substance of I AM.

"What is Truth?" Truth is always silent. It is beyond argument, dialectics, theories, dogmas, and creeds. Truth is an inner experience, an inner awareness, or feeling whereby you taste and touch reality for yourself. Your consciousness determines all your experiences and your relationship with the external world and all people. The Bible says, "I AM the Truth." The Presence of God (I AM) in you is the real Truth, the Changeless Reality within all of us. Truth is the subjective factor which is the real cause of all our experiences. It is no use to argue that two and two are not four. Truth permits no argument. Truth is.

Do not think for one moment, even though you are innocent of what you are saying, that it is an idle word. Because why? You are God (I AM), and God's (I AM) words cannot return unto him empty. They must accomplish that which he purposed and "prosper in the thing for which he sent it." So, even though you are ignorant of the Law, you are the operant power, operating that Law of which you may be totally unaware, but there is no excuse. You will still reap the results.

Now, if you test God (I AM) and prove to yourself that imagination does create reality, tell others. If they try it and it works for them, does it really matter what the world thinks? If they think the idea is insane, it won't be the first time. They thought Einstein was insane. There are those who think I am. That's perfectly all right, for the day will come when God (I AM) will reveal himself in each individual, and then that one will move from the state of Saul to Paul. There is no other God, for God became Man by assuming all of his human weaknesses and limitations. God (I AM) is not pretending he is you. When he became your breath, he had to take your unique qualities upon himself. That was his crucifixion. No man was nailed upon a cross bar; your body is the cross Christ wears. He is buried in you and will rise in you. His tomb is the human skull where he lays dreaming. So awake, you sleeper, who forgot eternity in the pursuit of the moment. Although this moment seems so real, you are its reality and the central being of scripture.

Whatever we do heartily and sincerely in the name of the I AM, carries with it the power of the I AM to accomplish . . a power from a higher source. All power is given to I AM. Doing all things "in his name" puts aside our mortal personality and lets the I AM do the work.

We treat of Spirit as the Active and the only Self-Conscious Principle. We define Spirit as the First Cause or God; the Absolute Essence of all that is. It is also called the great, or the Universal, I AM. When Moses asked God who he should tell the Children of Israel had sent him, the answer was, "Thus shalt thou say, I AM hath sent me unto you." The reason why "I AM" was given is because this is an absolute statement. Spirit is Conscious Mind, and is the Power Which knows Itself; It is conscious of Its own Being. The Spirit is Self-Propelling; it is Absolute and All. It is Self-Existent, and has all life within Itself. It is the Word, and the Word is volition. It has choice because It is Volition; It is will because It chooses; It is Free Spirit because It knows nothing outside Itself, and nothing different from Itself. Spirit is the Father-Mother God because It is the principle of Unity back of all things. The masculine and feminine principles both come from the One. Spirit is all Life, Truth, Love, Being, Cause and Effect; and is the only Power in the Universe that knows Itself.

Happiness, health, prosperity, are all at your command if you will but realize the truth. You must believe and feel your oneness with this supply . . then you can honestly say each day, "I AM Success," "I AM Health," "I AM Abundance," because you have made the connection and you have planted the seeds of health, success and abundance in your mind.

When someone born into poverty persists in dreaming he possesses great wealth and his dream comes true, his wealth seems perfectly natural to those who do not know his dream. You are dreaming. If you try to make your dream come true while doubting its possibility, you are heading toward a nervous breakdown. But if you go all out in your wonderful claim, you will fulfill it, for all things are possible to the God (I AM) you are, for you are the God (I AM) of whom the Bible speaks.

The visualizing and imaging faculties are the transcendent powers that cause the living Substance of God to flow freely, but It will fill only those molds prepared for it. As you mentally hold your picture in the dark room of the Silence, vigilantly guard against the intrusion of any vagrant thoughts that may distort your image. As your picture is impressed upon your consciousness, it becomes the center of attraction, and the I AM fills it with Substance. It becomes the property of the Universal Mind. At this point of development, Spirit specializes and differentiates your desire. The power which projects the originating Substance out from Itself is your I AM, and this Substance takes the specific shape which you have given it in your mind. The Universal becomes particular as you recognize that your mind is the particular center through which your I AM is seeking expression in a material sense.

The I AM in us is the only God we shall ever know. If we recognize It and accept It as health, It will manifest as an abundant health. If we recognize It and accept It as happiness, It will manifest as abundant happiness. If we recognize It and accept It as opulence, It will manifest as abundant prosperity. As we release this Divine Energy, It will become to us anything we believe It to be. Since we actually live and move in this Energy, there can be no thought of bringing God down to us from some high place in the sky, but rather of lifting our thought to the heavenly place in our own minds in which we may more fully comprehend Him. In the Silence, we cultivate a deep consciousness of unity with the Universal Creative Mind. We merge with It until It becomes our own Consciousness. We take from It as much as we are prepared to receive.

So, "Be still and know that I AM God." As we are told: "Unless you believe that I AM He, you will die in your sins."

So, the "I AM" in you is your own wonderful human imagination, and you can put it any place in the world. You need not be anchored to where your senses tell you that you are.

Men that you and I admire, if they were honest, would admit to implanting in our mind that which would belittle us and ennoble them. Many know what they are doing but they don't know Christ (I AM). If they did, they would know they do not have to belittle us to ennoble themselves. If you want to rise, you don't have to put another down in order to feel you have risen. Your reality is I AM.

Raise your consciousness and you raise yourself, but you haven't risen when you feel the need to push another down by claiming "I AM better than."

Tonight take this law and apply it. I promise you it will not fail. When you go to bed dwell in your own wonderful human imagination and say: "Thank you, Father" as though you were addressing another. You know you are thanking your human imagination, but while assuming you have what you want, thank your Father. You came out from the Father and came into the world. Now you are leaving the world and going to the Father. Eventually you will reach him, and when you do he is yourself. There is no other Father. There is no other God!

Jehovah (I AM) in the Hebrew is written Yahweh. Yah is the masculine and weh the feminine. The word is made up of masculine and feminine elements and represents the joining together of wisdom and love as a procreating nucleus. This is the Jehovah God who made the visible man, the man of self-consciousness. God manifest in substance is the Jesus Christ man. Elohim, universal Mind, creates, but Jehovah God forms. Being is without beginning or ending.

Universal Mind imaged itself in all that it created, and all its ideas are contained in the divine-idea man, which is Jehovah or the Christ. Jesus Christ is that perfection made manifest in man. Spiritual creating is ideation in Truth. The ideas of Divine Mind are contained potentially in substance, but until these ideas are consciously recognized by Jehovah God, the divine-idea man, they are not wholly manifest. All things exist as ideas, but these ideas are manifested only as spiritual man, becomes conscious of them.

The speed with which you make any demonstration will depend entirely upon the clarity of your mental picture. You cannot believe you are going to receive anything until you understand definitely what it is that you are going to receive. You must see the picture that you are presenting to Universal Mind very clearly. Not until your picture is clear do you have a good model or mold. The more perfect your picture, the more perfect your manifestation.

The I AM working through the imagination not only can create but can also control. Imagination is the permanizing force that takes an invisible idea and builds it into form. Jesus was able to explore every negative condition and image it into perfection. The Perfect Man is created in the image of the I AM; through Spiritual vision, you can restore your body to its spiritual purity and perfection.

The Universal Mind gives back to you what you deeply impress upon it. In the Silence, you are working in a spiritual foundry in which Universal Substance takes definite shape. If you are careless in your model or pattern, your product will be imperfect.

All negative thoughts and suggestions are recognized by you as illusions of power, for after all, there is only One Power . . God (I AM), the Living Spirit Almighty within. This is the argumentative method used in prayer and practiced by Quimby one hundred years ago, which enables you to come to a conclusion or verdict in your own mind of the availability of the Omnipotence of God (I AM) or Good at all times, in all emergencies, and in every crisis. As fear falls away, faith and confidence fill the mind; then you become united with your desire, and its fruition and blessings appear in your life.

Wherever you go, you are always imagining. You cannot leave the Lord behind you. You cannot sit here and wish imagination away as you can the body. I can stand here and assume that I am at the end of the room and imagine that I am looking at this one. But where am I? I AM in imagination. I can look at the body as something that I have put away for a while. I return to it. But I can't put away imagination. I cannot get away from the Lord, because, being all imagination, I must be wherever He is in imagination. So, if I now, in imagination feel things as I desire them to be, that's the Lord doing it. And because "All things are possible to the Lord," I must believe in me; I must believe it is the Lord (I AM) doing it.

I AM is the Super Mind, the sum total of God-Consciousness; the action of this mind is always within and upon Itself. It is the complement of the other two minds and the container of both. The three in reality are one. There is only one mind, the Universal Mind of God. Mind and Consciousness are interchangeable terms. Conscious and subconscious are two names for the One Mind. Subconscious and subjective mean the same thing . . the mind and the law of the soul.

Unlimited power is available to man as he consciously uses the creative force. The I AM which we discover in our own consciousness is the Principle we use in our work in the Silence. Both conscious and subjective minds are the instruments of the I AM. I AM is the perfect and full expression of invisible Spirit. It is the Universal Mind in action. I AM is health. I AM is prosperity. I AM is success. The I AM is the Principle and Power of God and the invisible power of man.

Don't wait for God (I AM) to do something. God (I AM) will do nothing for you except through your own thought. God (I AM) has given you everything. You are here to awaken through your mind, feeling, and consciousness. The transformation you are seeking you give to yourself psychologically and emotionally. The phrase born of the flesh means the mind saturated with world beliefs and opinions. You are born of the flesh if you let the world-mind and the race-belief govern you. Turn within and let your mind be governed by God's ideas (I AM). You will then be born of the spirit.

Tonight when you go to bed just say: "I AM." Add any condition you want to that I AM and believe it. Speak to your imagination as though you are speaking to the God who created the universe and sustains it, for you are. When you imagine something ask yourself who is imagining it, and you will say: "I AM." That's God's name forever and ever. Imagine and fall asleep imagining. Believe that all things are possible to your own wonderful human I AMness. Test yourself! You don't need to get down on your knees and pray to anyone on the outside. There is no need to cross yourself before any icon, for the Lord is your human imagination, your consciousness, your own wonderful I AMness. Nothing can ever cease to be, for God . . he who is in you as your consciousness . . created it in love.

Do you know what you want? I will tell you a simple way to get it. Simply catch the feeling that you have it and sustain that feeling. Persist in acknowledging the joy of fulfillment. In your imagination tell your friends your good news. Hear their congratulations, then allow him who heard your friends and felt your joy of fulfillment, bring it into your world, for he who can do all these things is within you as your own wonderful I AMness, your Imagination, your consciousness. That is God. Test God, for he will not fail you. Then, when he proves himself in performance, tell a friend, and continue telling others as you exercise this law. And walk knowing all the other I AM statements are yours.

Prove this in the world of shadows and you will prove the other in the world of reality. Your I AMness is the true eternal reality. Living in a world of shadows, as you declare your I AMness you are declaring eternal truth. When you say, "I AM the resurrection," that is eternal truth. "I AM the life" is eternal truth, as well as "I AM the way." All of these bold certainties preceded with the "I AM" are eternal truths. So, do not listen to anyone who screams at you from their tower of Babel and tells you of another way, for there is no other way. You don't have to give up meat or only eat fish on Friday in order to enter the way, for the way to the cause of all life is within you. Believe in your I AMness for there is no other God.

As the Word, you sent yourself into the world to fulfill all that you said you would. In the beginning you were the Word which was with God and was God. You are the Word which went forth from God's mouth and will not return void, but must accomplish that which you purposed and prosper in the thing for which you were sent. Coming out from the knowledge of being the Father, you brought with you the pattern of salvation. This you will fulfill, as it is this pattern that takes you back to the knowledge of being the Father you have been seeking.

You came out from yourself and entered the world of men by falling asleep to your true awareness. You will return to that awareness when you learn to trust the one and only God, who is your own wonderful human imagination. Forget all the little isms; there is only God! When you say I AM, you are speaking as God. Add any word and you have placed a limit on an infinite being. That which is unlimited, abides by his own law and becomes that which he believes himself to be . . whether it be unwanted, sick, helpless, or poor. Believe in a world of your own creation, and . . because all things are possible to imagine . . the moment you become aware of anything, you have given it the power to project itself on your screen of space.

What we call your mind and my mind are two manifestations or expressions of the One Mind. We do not say you have "an air" and I have "an air," or that a fish has "a water." There is one water in which fishes live; one air which we breathe; one Mind of which we are all a part. I AM is the Omnipresent, Universal Mind of God. It is the Principle of divine Unity underlying all creation; when Self conscious in man. There is no separation in Spirit; the individual mind can never be separated from the Universal Mind. I AM is Universal Mind. I AM is Life. I AM is Power. I AM is Health. I AM is Wealth. I AM is Success. I AM is Everything I am or can be, for I AM the I AM! To him that hath (the consciousness of I AM) shall be given; to him that hath not shall be taken away even that which he hath. It is one thing to say that we believe in God and quite another to be conscious of God.

If you think in terms of one little being called Jesus Christ, you miss the truth completely; for Jesus Christ is your own wonderful human imagination who is God (I AM) himself. When you imagine a state, God (I AM) has imagined it; and just as a sound brings a response, your world will respond by playing the part it must play to bring about fulfillment.

By purity of life we prepare the physical temple, and by deep devotion and holy aspiration we stir the depths of the soul into intense activity, and become a magnet for the indwelling Spirit. The soul is of the Creator; it came from that Infinite Source, and through it the spirit will express to the mind and body. The soul in its incarnation into a form of flesh is like a seed that has been sown in the earth. It must be watered by our thoughts of recognition and quickened by our deep feelings of love for the Creator. It has an affinity only for the truth of the Creator's love; the thoughts and feelings generated by earthly things becloud its faculties and hinder it from receiving its daily sustenance from the I AM within. If the mind of a person is centered wholly upon material things, the soul becomes isolated from the Creator.

Now, the words "God" and "Lord" mean I AM! Awareness is the foundation of all life, while the words God and Lord cover it up, like a mask. Rather than calling upon the Lord's name, call with his name. To do that you must say I AM! And because all things are possible to God, anything can be called forth with his name. The minute consciousness is connected to desire, you have called it forth with God's name. If your desire is for wealth, fame, or health, call it forth by claiming: I AM famous, I AM wealthy, or I AM healthy.

An imaginal act is an immediate objective fact.

Functioning on low intensities as we are, an imaginal act is realized in a time process. And so every vision as it stands there I assume that I AM; but at the moment reason denies and my senses deny, but I assume that I AM. And if I assume it and it seems to me real and natural, when I break the spell I know I have planted it, and then it has its own appointed hour. Every vision has its own period of gestation, as we are told by the prophet: "It has its own appointed hour, it ripens, it will flower, if it seems slow then wait, it is sure, it will not be late." If you see it clearly in your mind's eye, if you were really in the image, it will become just as objective as this room is now . . and again I am speaking from experience.

Sitting in my chair at home or reclining on a couch or in my bed, suddenly . . without my eyes being physically open . . I see a world that I would not see if I know where I am physically, and I can't deny it. It's just as real as you are. It's objective, it is seemingly solidly real, and consciousness follows vision and I step into the world that I am observing. And stepping into my image it closes around me, and this world which is seemingly the only world I should know is shut out, and I am part of the world I contemplated, I am in it. I explore that world and it is just as solidly real as this world.

Jesus, your I AM, is the Word that was sent to transform you into himself. He is the creator of it all, for although you seem so limited and unable to create anything here, you can see everything made perfect in your imagination. You can imagine a state, remain faithful to it and it will be made alive for you. Now, if I AM made everything and you know you imagined it before it appeared, and it appeared because you imagined it, then you have found Jesus Christ to be your own wonderful human imagination.

Through the imagining power of Divine Mind, Spirit propels Itself into creation. Will power is never creative; to suppose that God had to will things into being would be to suppose an opposite or contending force to God. The Substance that you have extracted from your original and associated ideas must now be reproduced in form. It must be translated from the invisible into the visible. It must be materialized so that you can possess it in a tangible way. Each step brings you nearer to the object of your desire. The Universal Substance that you are causing to stand around you idea, whose center is I AM, is permeable, impressible, plastic, retentive and sensitive. The I AM, or Spirit, will vitalize any picture that you visualize. It will draw from the Universal Substance whatever is necessary for its material fulfillment.

There is no other God other than he who is your own wonderful human imagination. Turn to any other and you have turned to a false God. Now, make no graven image of God. "I AM" has no face. Unnumbered artists have drawn pictures of what they conceive Jesus to be, but he has no face. He is simply "I AM." I did not know that the story of Jesus Christ was mine. I did not know Jesus interpreted the Old Testament with himself as the very center of it; that the human imagination . . our human I AMness . . was He. But now I know that there never was another Jesus and there never will be another, and those who teach another are false teachers teaching a false Christ.

Oftentimes man forgets the Source of his power and becomes drunk with power, so to speak. In other words, he misuses the law and selfishly takes advantage of his fellow man. We find that many times men in high places become conceited, opinionated, and arrogant. This is all due to ignorance of the law. The law is that power, security, and riches are not to be obtained externally. They must come from the treasure-house of consciousness. If you remain in tune with the Infinite, you discover that you are always drinking of the wine of life, love, joy, and happiness. To the spiritually-minded man, God (I AM) is the Eternal Now and his good is present at every moment of time and point of space.

Now I know I AM the center of creative power. The day will come when you too will awaken and exercise your creative power, knowingly. That is our destiny, for we all will awaken as God and use this power to create in the true sense of the word. Try to remember that there is no limit to God's creative power, or your power of belief. Persuade yourself that things are as you desire them to be. Fall asleep in that assumption, as that is your act of faith. Tomorrow the world will begin to change, to make room for the garment of your assumption.

If there is only one cause, then he who quelled the wind and the sea is the one who caused the storm. There cannot be another. If there is confusion in your life, and you resolve it in your imagination, and the world bears witness to what you have done . . you caused the change. And since there is no other cause, then did you not cause the confusion also? There is only one God and Father of us all who is above all, through all, and in all. If He is in every being who says I AM, and there is only one God, no one can accuse another; for God's name is not he is, but I AM. No matter what appears on the outside, I am its cause. Assume full responsibility for the things you observe, and if you do not like what you see, know you have the power to change them. Then exercise that power and you will observe the change you caused. If you are truly willing to assume that responsibility, you are set free.

Do you know what you want from life? You can be anything you want to be if you know who you are. Start from the premise, "I AM all imagination and pass through states," for eternity (all things) exist now! Having experienced a state and moved into another one you may think the former state has ceased to be, but all states are eternal, they remain forever. Like the mental traveler that you are, you pass through states either wittingly or unwittingly, but your individual identity is forever. Whether you are rich or poor, you retain the same individual identity when you move from one state into another. If you are not on guard, you can be persuaded by the press, television, or radio, to change your concept of self and unwittingly move into an undesirable state. You can move into many states and play many parts, but as the actor, you do not change your identity. When you are rich, you are the same actor as when you are poor. These are only different parts you are playing.

Claim what you want to be aware of here and now, and . . although your reasonable mind denies it and your senses deny it . . if you will assume it, with feeling, your inward activity, established and perpetuated, will objectify itself in the outside world . . which is nothing more than your imaginal activity, objectified. To attempt to change the circumstances of your life before you change its imaginal activity (I AM), is to labor in vain.

The thought which we must keep in mind is that God Consciousness does not change or add anything to us. Our only purpose is to reveal the Life Principle and Power of the Universal Mind, God. When we treat, or attempt to move negative conditions such as disease and poverty, we are recognizing two powers and binding the negative conditions to us. We are unconsciously admitting that the good we seek does not exist. Jesus said, I AM come not to destroy, but to fulfill. Even a thought about lack, or a desire to add substance to ourselves, is to discredit the Mind which is the Substance of all things. The positive qualities of the I AM will always become visible when we drop from our consciousness the belief in the negative qualities.

I urge you to use your imagination for everything that is lovely and loving. I don't care what your desire may be . . your imagination will give it to you, for the human imagination is the divine body the world calls Jesus. Because you can imagine and I can imagine, we are members of that one divine body, and all things are possible to him. There is not a thing impossible to God (I AM). All you need do is imagine its fulfillment! Faith is an experiment which ends as an experience. Experiment by believing you already have all that you desire, and you will have the experience.

"I AM the beginning and the end. There is nothing to come that has not been and is." So look upon creation as finished . . and you and I are only selectors of that which is. By selectors I mean that you and I have the privilege (we may not exercise it) but it is our privilege to select that aspect of reality to which we will respond, and in responding to it, we bring it into existence for ourselves. Not knowing that we are so privileged, we simply go through the world reflecting the circumstances of life, not realizing we have the power to create or to out picture the circumstance of life.

As we vibrate (think) in the Universal Mind, we have the consciousness of unity. Vibration is at the base of all form; it is independent of physical force. When we learn how to vibrate consciously in the Universal Mind, we shall know that we are one with the substance of I AM. The highest vibrations and the greatest power are silent. When we enter the Silence, we change our rate of vibration from the slow and negative to the fast and positive. We lose our sense of the personal as we merge with the impersonal I AM. Ye shall receive power when the Holy Spirit is come upon you. When we become one with Spirit, Spirit enters into us and we enter into it. It manifests through us as perfect being. Let there be Light. God thought and wrought. Then Word was spoken, that which was authoritatively affirmed was done, and there was Light.

God's revealed name to this world is "I AM." That is his great name. Can you say, "I AM?" That is God. What am I doing? I am thinking you are no good . . well, that is what you're doing, that is God in action. And do you know: you will live to see the day you are right. So "I AM" doing what? Anything in this world, all things are possible to God. When you say: "I don't believe so and so." Perfectly all right, that's your privilege, but who is not believing it? "I AM," you say . . well, that is God. Don't believe it. "I am no good, I can't make a living." Well that is your privilege; believe it and may I tell you how true God is: he'll prove it. Finally you are relieved and you will say to me: "I told you it's no good." Can't you realize that you are setting it in motion and you were fertilizing it in your world, for God's only revealed name is "I AM." So, what are you imagining?

The omnipotent Will of the Creator is holding worlds and solar systems in obedience to a harmonious order. You stand in the highest order of created beings, and you have the ability to come in direct contact with the divine Will, to the end that It may express Its purpose of perfection through your whole nature. Develop the divine Will within you by expressing It. You can cultivate such a mighty force of will by the constant assertion, "I AM, I will," that every temptation will be overcome and every bad habit transformed into good by the awakening of this mighty attribute of your divinity.

God spoke to Jacob and told him not to fear to go down into Egypt, because He (God) would go with him and bring him out again after he had become a great nation. The descent into the land of Egypt of Jacob and his sons, together with the possessions that they had accumulated in Canaan, their wives, children, goods, flocks, and herds, symbolizes to us the unification of the I AM with all the faculties of the mind and of the life energy and substance of the whole man with the body. This happy result is brought about by the action of the faculty of imagination (all dwelt together "in the land of Goshen," which signifies unity). This new state of mind becomes a part of the permanent consciousness in the new land. "And Joseph shall put his hand upon thine eyes" means that through the faculty of imagination the perception of the other faculties is quickened and increased.

Unless we hold ourselves in the positive attitude of our own greatness, the opportunity for success on any line of experience will be lessened. Self-view must be enlarged that Self may behold itself the truly potent, powerful agent it is. When this is done both mind and body will become potent in activity. No one can afford to limit his possibilities by denying the I AM . . Love . . by agreement with appearances.

Although this world appears so very real, it is a vision.
"All that you behold, though it appears without, it is within, in your Imagination of which this world of mortality is but a shadow." If life is in God and God is your imagination, then what the world calls life is only an activity of your imagination. If you stop imagining and arrest that which seems to be animated and independent of your perception, you will prove to yourself that it can be done. Then you will know who Christ is, for you will have discovered that "In him is life and his life is the light of men." God animates Man within himself. Although humanity appears to be independent, with life in themselves, their life is but an activity of imagination, for that is what I AM!

There is no more important part in the understanding of the Law of Abundance, than to understand man's active, conscious part. By this I mean to be conscious that man's part is to decide how the Divine Energy, "I AM," will manifest in the realm of visibility. We must remember that we have nothing to do with the working of the Law but we have some conscious part in just how that Law will work. God (I AM) as the Universal Energy flows on and on as silent, impersonal, omnipotent Power until it reaches a place where consciousness is manifest.

So, you either believe in your own wonderful human imagination or you do not, for that is Christ (I AM). An event took place 2,000 years ago, but it didn't take place once, never to take place again. His birth is taking place in the lives of everyone who hears and believes. So what must you do? Believe in him whom he has sent. I did not come into the world to make you think I am a holy man, but to tell you that I have awakened from the dream of life. I have finished the race. I have fought the good fight, and I have kept the faith. It doesn't really matter when I drop this garment, for this world is over for me. I will tell you of my experiences while I am here, in the hope that you will believe . . not in Neville, but in your own wonderful human imagination whom you sent! Your true name is I AM, and your creative power is called Jesus Christ. Because all things are made by your imagination, test yourself and see. Put your powerful imagination to the test.

As I speak my word and decree a thing, it is done in divine right order and right on time. God (I AM) is my Source and my true supply. Universal Intelligence is responding to the claim I am making, and is manifesting my desire into form, as I speak. This is certain, I am certain, and my faith is absolute. It is done, and I say: "Thank you, God, and so it is."

Your I AMness is He. Say: "I AM secure, I AM wealthy, I AM free." This may not be true based upon your senses, but I am simply asking you to say the words, for the moment you do you are subjectively appropriating security, wealth, and freedom. Reason will try to take these from you, so I ask you to play a little game with me. Go through the door and walk as though you are secure, wealthy, and free. Sleep this night as though it were true. If you do, you will not fall asleep seeing the world as you did last night, you will see it differently. If this morning someone gave you a check for $20,000 and you deposited it to your account, you would be $20,000 richer, therefore you could not sleep tonight as you did before. Now, without waiting for someone to physically give you the money, go to bed as though it were true. Put Christ to the extreme test. If all things are possible to God and if all things are possible to the believer, can you believe? I am not saying you will succeed the first night, or even the second. Having been trained to accept only what your reason and senses dictate, you may find it difficult, almost impossible, to believe what you could believe . . but you can!

I AM, the two most powerful words, spoken or thought, for what we attach to I AM is given to us, what we attach to I AM is added unto us. This is the "asking in his name".

Now, if Christ is the one quoted as radiating from within you, and by him all things are made and without him is not anything made that is made (even the bad), then you must find him. If there is only one maker, is it not He who made your awful day, your awful month, your awful year? If you are brutally honest with yourself, you will admit that what happened was related to your imaginal acts. When you recognize and acknowledge this, you have found him. And because He is a person and you are a person, you know exactly who He is. Now, walk with your head up high, knowing that you have learned from your mistakes; and from now on try to imagine the best as you perceive the best to be, knowing that these acts must project themselves in this world. Then you will awaken and rejoin the brothers, for "I AM not a God afar off, in me lo we are one, forgiving all evil and seeking no recognition." If we are one, why should I demand recognition? Why not forgive all, for they know not what they do.

Remove the word "if" from your vocabulary, as it is not productive of that which you would like to reap. "If" puts everything in the past or future tense, and I always experience what I believe I AM. I AM is not future tense. Getting well is not being well. I must believe that I AM already what I want to be.

When you imagine a state, do you believe that the scene has the power to externalize itself? Or do you feel you must pray to a being on the outside for help? I tell you: there is no being on the outside. The creative power of the world is housed within you now. Sit down and imagine a state of confidence that it must externalize itself. Believe that because all things are possible to imagine, the state you have imagined must become an external fact. I have tried this time and time again, and it has always proved itself in performance. Now I share this knowledge with everyone who will listen. How many believe my words and put them into practice I do not know. I only know that man finds it hard to keep the tense. Religious leaders speak of God in the third person as if he were on the outside, yet I tell you he comes from within. When Moses heard the words: "I AM has sent me unto you," it seemed to come from without, yet it was whispered from within.

Let this be your daily affirmation; write it in your heart, "I AM one with the infinite riches of my subconscious mind. It is my right to be rich, happy, and successful. Money flows to me freely, copiously, and endlessly. I AM forever conscious of my true worth. I give of my talents freely, and I AM wonderfully blessed financially. It is wonderful!"

There is only one door into the sheepfold and that door is "I AM". The supreme effort that God ever made to reveal Himself to us in the present tense came through Jesus. So Jesus comes affirming God as the eternal contemporary, forever and forever. If tomorrow you have a child or a grandchild, they are going to say, "I AM". It is contemporary . . forever contemporary, and eternally contemporary. It wasn't that he was . . it is always "I AM". And so for one to declare, "I AM" . . and simply name it and sleep as though it were true . . there is no power in the world that could stop it.

Use this Statement: " 'I AM' the fulfilled activity and sustaining power of every constructive thing I desire." Use it as a general statement, for the sustaining power is in everything that there is. "'I AM' here and 'I AM' there" in whatever you want to accomplish is a splendid way to feel that you are using the One Activity, and you thus rise above the consciousness of separation.

A friend of mine, maybe, is unwell; or maybe he's unemployed, or maybe he is not earning enough to meet the obligations of life. All right, he is in me. As I think of him, he's in me. He need not be physically present for me to think of him; he's in me. I think of him; I conjure him. Well, can I change his entire picture in me? I assume that he is talking to me, and he's telling me that he has never had more, he has never felt better; and as I believe in what I am seeing in my own mind's eye, . . I believe in him. That is Christ in me, and all things are possible to Christ. Well then, test it and see if it works. See if you do not see him in the not too distance future earning more, looking better; and everything in the world that you have done within you, he responds to. He need not praise you or thank you.

You don't need his praise; you don't need his thanks. You don't need confirmation from him, other than he does conform to what you have done in yourself concerning him. You ask no one to thank you. Thank nothing. You are simply exercising the power of God within you. "And the power of God and the wisdom of God is Jesus Christ". And there is nothing in the world but God. It is all God in you "pushed out," and God is your own wonderful human imagination. He can't be closer. God is never so far off as even to be near, for nearness implies separation. He's not separated. God actually, literally became as I AM, that I may be as He is.

He is not something on the outside. No matter how near He is, He can't even touch me. He actually became me, with all of my weaknesses, all of my limitations; and now I am trying to struggle within myself to find out who I AM, . . and that's His name. My name is in Him. What's your name? "Go and say I AM has sent you." "Is that your name?" "Yes, forever and forever it is my name." "What name? Jehovah?" "No." "The Lord?" "No, I AM." That's His name. That is His name forever and forever.

So I say to all: the one who makes everything is the human imagination. This may seem cruel to one who is now experiencing pain, but it is true. I have suffered. I have known physical pain. Even though I may say I caught the flu, I know I caught it within me. I read the paper where I learned that 50 per cent of the people had the flu, and . . becoming a statistic . . I made it fifty-one. I have experienced its aches and pains, and learned a lesson. Now I know that even though I have experienced the drama of Jesus Christ (I AM), I am still subject to everything man is subject to. I know that I cannot point to any other cause other than my own imagination, as cause cannot come from the outside. If I am in pain, the cause is mine. We are told in Galatians that God . . your imagination (I AM) . . is not mocked. That as you sow, so shall you reap.

Everyone automatically attracts to himself just what he is, and you may set it down that wherever you are, however intolerable the situation may be, it is just where you belong. There is no power in the Universe but yourself that can get you out of it. Someone may help you on the road to realization, but substantiality and permanence can come only through the consciousness of your own life and thought. Man must bring himself to a point where there is no misfortune, no calamity, no accident, no trouble, no confusion; where there is nothing but plenty, peace, power, Life and Truth.

He should definitely, daily, using his own name, declare the Truth about himself, realizing that he is reflecting his statements into Consciousness, and that they will be operated upon by It. This is called, in mysticism, High Invocation; invoking the Divine Mind; implanting within It seeds of thought relative to one's self. And this is why some of the teachers of older times used to teach their pupils to cross their hands over their chests and say: "Wonderful, wonderful, wonderful me!" definitely teaching them that, as they held themselves, so they would be held. "Act as though I AM and I will Be."

One of the ancient sayings is that, "To the man who can perfectly practice inaction, all things are possible." This sounds like a contradiction until one gets down to the inner teachings; for it is only when one completely practices inaction that he arrives at the point of the true actor. For he then realizes that the act and the actor are one and the same, that cause and effect are the same; which is simply a different way of saying: "Know the Truth and the Truth shall make you free." To reduce the whole thing to its simplest form, whatever one reflects into Mind will be done.

The creator of the world works in the depth of your soul, underlying all of your faculties, including perception, and streams into your surface mind least disguised in the form of creative fancy. Watch your thoughts, and you will catch Him in the act of creating, for He is your very Self! Every moment of time you are imagining what you are conscious of, and if you do not forget what you are imagining and it comes to pass, you have found the creative cause of your world. Because God is pure imagination and the only creator, if you imagine a state and bring it to pass, you have found Him. Remember: God is your consciousness, your I AM; so when you are imagining, God is doing it. If you imagine and forget what you imagine, you may not recognize your harvest when it appears. It may be good, bad, or indifferent, but if you forget how it came into being, you have not found God.

While the newer lands of the West, with their active pioneers in activity, have been pushing forward toward material advancement and progress, India has been resting quietly, dreaming of that which lies back of the material world, and under and above physical existence. To the Hindu mind the physical and material world is more or less of an illusion, inasmuch as it passes away almost while it is being formed, and is a thing of the moment merely . . while the spiritual world is the real one and the one to which the mind of man may most properly be turned.

Mind you, we are merely stating the fact and existing conditions that you may understand them, not as urging that the above method is the better. For, to be frank with you, we consider the general tendency of the Hindu mind to be as much "one-sided" as that of the Western world . . the one leans to the "I AM" side, ignoring the "I Do" side; while the other places entire dependence upon the "I Do" phase, almost entirely ignoring the "I AM" phase. The one regards the side of Being, and ignores the side of Action; while the other regards Action as the essential thing, ignoring the vital importance of Being.

To the Western world the Physical is the dominant phase . . to the East the Metaphysical holds the lead. The thinking minds of both East and West clearly see that the greatest progress in the future must come from a combining of the methods of the two lands, the Activity of the West being added to the Thought of the East, thus inspiring the old lands into new activities and energy; while to the Western activity must be added the spirituality and "soul-knowledge" of the East, in order that the rampant materiality may be neutralized and a proper balance maintained.

No one would ever agree with another as to what is right and what is wrong, for we all have different values. What is right to one is wrong to another. We came down into the world of death because we ate of the tree of knowledge of good and evil, and we are told that the only thing that displeases God is the eating of that tree, and unbelief. If you think another is the cause of your misfortune, you are sinning and missing your mark in life. There is only one cause for all of the phenomena of your life, and that is God, whose eternal name is I AM. When you really believe this, you will not deny the harvest you are reaping. It may be unpleasant, but you will know that it couldn't happen unless you sowed it, so accept your harvest and then plant something lovely in its place. Never deny that one and only cause, which is your own wonderful human imagination!

At the end of the drama it is said that one who knew Jesus betrayed him. Now, in order to betray someone, you must know his secret! So the one who knows the secret betrays him. That one is self! God is self-revealed. Unless God (I AM) reveals himself to you, how will you ever know him? Turning to those who did not know him, Jesus said: "Now that you have found me, do not let me go, but let all these go." Let every belief of a power on the outside go, but do not let the belief in your powerful imagination go . . for truth is within you. When you find the Maker (I AM) in yourself, then no matter what arguments the priesthoods may give, do not believe them, for the Christ you seek is the human imagination.

Tomorrow you may forget and be penetrated by rumors which disturb your body and cause you to suffer. When this happens you must reestablish your harmony by imagining things are as you desire them to be. Living in this wonderful world, we cannot stop the penetration. To perceive another, that other must first penetrate your brain; therefore, he is within you as well as on the outside and independent of your perception. Cities, mountains, rivers and streams, must first penetrate your brain for you to be aware of them. At that moment of awareness they are within you, even though they still maintain a certain independence of your perception and are without. Treat this inner penetration seriously and you will discover all you need to do is adjust your thinking. That you are all imagination and must be wherever you think you are. If you want to contact a friend, simply adjust yourself to his community by making there . . here, and then . . now. Visit him in his home by penetrating it within yourself. Give him your message and see his eyes light up with the pleasure of your words.

If, in our solitude, we experience in our imagination what we would experience in reality had we achieved our goal, we will in time, become transformed into the image of our ideal. "Be renewed in the spirit of your mind . . put on the new man . . speak every man truth with his neighbor." The process of making a "Fact of being a fact of consciousness" is by the "renewing of our mind." We are told to change our thinking. But we can't change our thought unless we change our ideas. Our thoughts are the natural outpouring of our ideas, and our innermost ideas are the man himself. The end of longing is always to be . . not to do. Be still and know "I AM that which I desire." Strive always after being. External reforms are useless if your heart is not reformed. Heaven is entered not by curbing our passions; but rather, by cultivating our virtues. An old idea is not fickly forgotten, it is crowded out by new ideas. It disappears when a wholly new and absorbing idea occupies our attention. Old habits of thinking and feeling . . like dead oak leaves . . hang on till they are pushed off by new ones.

In the Heart of man's being, where he is one with the Father, the Father says, "I AM that power, substance and intelligence which is the fulfillment of your every desire." In Soul, the question is asked, "What do you desire?" In Mind, it is required, "Believe ye have that which ye desire." In Expression, it is promised, "And ye shall have the fulfillment of your desire." As has been before stated, this is a creative law, the law of bringing forth, and in operation is exactly the same as that used upon the physical plane when father and mother conceive a child, the body of which is given form within the matrix of the mother, and in fullness of time is brought to birth. Even so the Spirit (father) and Soul (mother) conceive what is to be brought forth, and this seed idea is held within the matrix of the soul, the mind, until in fullness of time it is produced in form, or delivered upon the physical plane.

It is now easy to see that your desire in the without must through "the silence," or in prayer be carried to the inner sanctuary of the soul ("thy closet") and there placed as a definite request before the Father . . the I AM. This is "asking." The Spirit asks, "What shall I do for thee?" You answer by naming your desire . . by asking.

Lifted to the spiritual plane, your request is there quickened by the Spirit and becomes a conception in your soul. Now it is a conceived idea, . . . a seed planted in the soil of your soul. As any other seed, it will germinate, develop first in the invisible, and in "fullness of time" come forth.

The mind, conscious of this, expects the fulfillment, as does a mother her child, or a farmer his harvest. This is "believing." It is "holding in mind" the form of the perfected expression. The mother believes she has her child, even when it is being formed in the invisible. The farmer believes he has his harvest, even while it is growing beneath the soil.

We must "believe we have" our demonstration while it is being formed for us in the inner realms of consciousness, for it is "believing we have" that holds definitely in mind the form of our desire, and gives it the desired form. When we believe we have, seeing in faith, "the invisible," we have.

In fullness of time, this thought form is delivered upon the physical plane. As a mother's birth effort delivers her child, so you through physical effort perfect your demonstration. It requires strength to speak and act in a way that is true to the conception, and to carry out the idea held in mind. The idea of health and the thought form of health must not be denied by the action of sickness or by resorting to external means to try to get well. The thought form is perfect health now.

If the soul conception is abundance, the action must carry out that idea. The spirit of the action must conform to the image. Until abundance manifests the amount of expenditure need not be increased, but the spirit of the mind must be one of richness, and what is spent must be allowed to leave the hands cheerfully and willingly in no consciousness of loss or of self-denial, but rather in the attitude of trust and thanksgiving because of the ever present supply now being made manifest. Be true. Spirit, soul, mind and body must agree to bring forth even as you have conceived, exactly "according to your faith." "Ye shall reap in due time (the time of fulfillment) if ye faint not. "Be not faithless, but believing.'

In the 2nd chapter of the Book of Jeremiah, the Lord said: "I planted you a pure seed, O Israel. How did you become degenerate?" I will tell you how! By going after foreign gods; by worshipping the gods of astrology, numerology, wealth, or so-called important people. By believing in things on the outside and seeing other causes for the phenomena of your life and not the only cause, who is God, your own wonderful human imagination, whose name is I AM! One day you will awaken to discover that you are the one and only God. But you aren't going to rob anyone, for it takes all your brothers, together, to form the one pyramid, and when this is accomplished the top stone will be put in place.

So tonight I ask you to exercise your own wonderful human imagination. Since your friends are only yourself out pictured, put them in a glorious light. Don't justify their actions by saying: "It serves them right", because all things exist in you. There is no one out there, but all in you! So if you fail a thousand times, saying: "How often Lord must I forgive my brother who sinned against me?" the answer will come: "Seventy times seven." May I tell you: you can't say "sin" in any other way than as recorded in the 51st Psalm, the 4th verse: "Against thee, O Lord, thee only have I sinned and done that which is evil in thy sight; therefore thy justification is in order."

Who is this being in whom I have sinned? His name is I AM! How have I sinned against thee and thee only? By seeing someone in my world that is in need and allowing them to remain there, for I cannot sin against another as I am the one seeing it. So I must change and represent him to myself as someone I desire to see. And I must persist in that belief until he conforms to the image I have created. That is what you are called upon to do, for you were made subject unto vanity and live alone in your world, so if you desire it to change, you alone must change it and live in the state of the desired change. I know this from experience, because the night that I was lifted up to the state of perfection I came upon this infinite sea of human imperfection, and as I glided by all were made perfect in harmony with that state to which

I was lifted. So you must lift yourself to the state you desire your world to reflect, because everything in it is yourself made visible. The whole vast world is projecting God, and God's name is I AM! Believe my visions, for they have never betrayed me. I may betray my vision by not accepting its message, but when I was lifted up I was shown that everyone I encounter is myself. And when I represent that seeming other to myself as I would like him to be, to the degree I persist in that assumption, he conforms to that state.

There is a sense of being aroused by the assertion "I AM", which, when exercised, gives one a feeling of conscious power. At first this is felt more sensibly if the eyes are closed and the whole mind is concentrated on the assertion of being, in the use of the words, "I AM". Persistent affirmation of positive states of mind polarizes, or draws to a center, the nebulous thought elements of mind, so that one gains a personal grasp of one's self and feels positively powerful to be and do and overcome. Practiced in the, morning for a while, it gives one a sense of poise that remains all through the day. In my own nature, personal consciousness was evolved from a state of subjective vagueness to a state of objective power through methods of mental assertiveness. The development of positiveness will give life, virility, and enduring quality to all your physical and mental work. "Nothing is at last sacred," says Emerson, "but the integrity of your own mind."

Word, thought, idea and Spirit-power bear exactly the same relation to each other that the key, hammer, string and vibration bear to each other in a piano. The vibration, or power within the string is released as sound to the ear only as the key in connection with it is struck. The key C moves the hammer C which touches the string C and releases the vibration C. In no other way can that particular tone be brought forth. If we want the tone C, we must be particular to strike the key C. In the same way, the word health moves the thought health, and awakens the idea health until the vibration or feeling of health is released in consciousness. It is for this reason that the weak are told to say "I AM strong." Strength is what the weak wish to experience, therefore they must say it and think it and in exact fulfillment of the law of faith they will feel it, but they will not do so as long as they persist in saying "weak."

These true words, or words declaring the truth of Being, are the "keys of the kingdom" to which Jesus referred when he told Peter, the man of faith, that they would be given to him. They are given to every faithful soul who will lift the consciousness above the testimony of the senses, or the opinions of others, and voice the Truth from the prompting of the Spirit within. In no other way can the "church" of Christ which is the "temple of the body" be built, for it must be formed from within, but can be only as the word which calls it forth is spoken from without. The kingdom of heaven is within, and the keys which unlock this kingdom to the consciousness of man are the good words or words of God which we speak. We must speak the words that are true of Being, then will the true become manifest, and the false will pass away.

Often we miss the fruit of faith because we have not continued in faith, or awaited the fulfillment of faith. No farmer would plant his grain and not await his harvest. Instead he would make preparation for his harvest. He would plant his seed believing that he would receive. Even so a mother who has conceived a child trusts that interior growth which takes place and which is hid from her view, and prepares for the birth of the child, believing she has received. So, when we speak the word of Truth which is the seed of the ideal we wish to see manifest, we must believe we have, and with no doubt in the mind, trust that first growth which always takes place within, hid from view. Fear, doubt and uncertainty prevent the perfect "holding in mind" of the thing desired, and until it is established, or made firm, in mind it cannot take form in the external.

Just as a seed must be established in the earth before it will start to grow, so must an idea be established in mind before it will begin to express. A wavering mind is not established, and James tells us that in this consciousness we can never hope to receive from the Lord or from the outworking of the law. "Let him ask in faith nothing wavering. For he that wavereth is like a wave of the sea, driven with the wind and tossed, for let not that man think he shall receive anything of the Lord'"

Therefore be firm in speaking the word of truth for healing. Affirm that which is true in Being by speaking the true word which will unlock the inner kingdom of reality and establish its ideas in experience. When the word for the true condition has been spoken, claim the effect of that word, and be unmoved by any appearance to the contrary. From the moment the word of Truth is spoken, claim its full fruition, believing that you have received, and act in perfect accord with that belief. Action must carry out the spirit of the mind, . . not contradict it. It is this that builds the house, or establishes the body, so that nothing from without can affect it. From the moment you speak the word "health," hold it in mind, and act as though health is already received for in this way is the law of faith fulfilled.

Regardless of every appearance, claim that health is yours from the moment you ask the Father within to manifest as health, for the Father within, or this Infinite Power in the Heaven within, can no more avoid responding than the sound within the piano can help coming forth when the key is struck. For this reason it is written, "If you ask for bread, will he give you a stone?" He cannot give you a stone, for it is the nature of the Father to give you that for which you ask. "Ask and you shall receive, for everyone that asketh, receiveth."

I tell you: the only God in the universe is your own wonderful human imagination. When you say: "I AM," that is God. There is no other God other than he who is encased in the limitation of your little garment of flesh. How can you call upon him, when you do not believe you are he? And how can you believe in him of whom you have never heard? What preacher ever told you that your own wonderful human imagination is God? They paint a word picture of a god outside of you, but that is not the true God. And when someone comes and tells you who He really is, the idea is blasphemous.

No one wants to believe that he is creating the conditions of his life; but God (I AM) is the only causative power, as there is nothing but God. Everything is caused by Imagination. He is the only reality. So, how can you believe in him of whom you have never heard? And how can you hear of him unless there is a preacher? And how can there be a preacher unless he is sent?

How many people today can pinpoint their success or failure to their imagination? The average man will say: John Brown did it, or the storm, or the president. Only a few will confess that their success or failure was created in their imagination. But I tell you: Christ in you creates your life, for you are all imagination and your imagination can be used for good or for evil. When you think of God as a man of imagination, you are recognizing the power behind the mask God wears. Rather than giving credit to the mask, praise the wearer, who is Christ. It is Christ who erupts from within us. Christ is the one who bears the name I AM, which is what the words Jesus, Joshua, and Jehovah really mean.

Creation is finished and perfect. There is actually nothing to heal or be added from the outside. God is that which I AM; my purpose is not to demonstrate things, but to reveal, or to give out from my Center, what that Center is. I can do that only by keeping myself in absolute harmony with that which I AM. Acknowledge him in all the ways. I am saved from all untoward circumstances only by virtue of what I AM, by the Life Principle of the Universal Mind. I AM the way, the truth and the life. My mission is to cooperate with the Universal Consciousness in my own mind. The circumstances of my life will automatically express the harmonious action of my thought.

There is only one door into the sheepfold and that door is "I AM." The supreme effort that God ever made to reveal Himself to us in the present tense came through Jesus. So Jesus comes affirming God as the eternal contemporary, forever and forever. If tomorrow you have a child or a grandchild, they are going to say, "I AM." It is contemporary . . forever contemporary, and eternally contemporary. It wasn't that he was . . it is always "I AM." And so for one to declare, "I AM" . . and simply name it and sleep as though it were true . . there is no power in the world that could stop it.

"The Power of The I AM"

From

Walter Devoe's

"Mystic Words of Mighty Power"

The I is the man, the Self. This very short word has never yet been pronounced with even one-hundredth part of the force which belongs to it. I must take hold of my individuality and lift it out of the earth-mire into which it has been dragged by the earth's negatives.

I must lift it up and establish its identity in the world. I must stamp the impress of my personality on all my environments.

My I AM is the image and likeness of the great I AM. I will claim the power of the I AM.

I will attain to my highest aim, which is to hold myself in God. I will hold my I at the right hand, the positive side, of the Throne of Power.

I AM the personality of Power. I have won the victory by my own persistent efforts, God being my strength.

I have grown to my present degree of power out of latent Good or God.

My I AM is Master. I AM: I have gained the mastery.

I have demonstrated according to my will and wisdom. I can demonstrate more and more therefore I will not be subservient to anything.

I AM the highest expression of God. I AM the image of divine strength. I deny weakness; there is naught of it in me.

I have my origin in the Central Sun. I AM in the warmth or love of the life of the divine Sun.

I have gained the recognition of the truth and I AM positive to all things and substances that have not gained this recognition. This recognition is the key to the healing of the whole world and I hold it now within my conscious mind.

Healers must recognize in all patients the power of life over death, the power of positive over negative, and thus establish this positive condition within them. As they come to recognize the power of positive thought they will see that all must be taught to overcome.

Effort is necessary. Unceasing effort brings all the faculties and forces of the mind into activity.

The desire to overcome must be cultivated. The seeming difficulty of overcoming lies in the way of assuming the position of mastery.

The power of habit must be broken. All who wish to gain this high position must break through the habits of their old ways of believing. This should be done by and through exercising the force of the will.

When one gains the true understanding of his position as a wielder of the power of the divine Will, he must remember to use his will in breaking all conditions, for the will is the I, and this I is so great, by virtue of the power of God vested in it, that the rest of the personality is nothing in comparison with it.

Thus I must break the fixed habit of thought which, despite the intelligent understanding, still clings to the external part. The beliefs in the power of disease held by the race, and held by the conscious mind before it became aware of its mastery, are consolidated in the surface mind. Those beliefs and the cells in which they reside are but negative intelligence. They may be brought into subjection and their tendencies redeemed through the exercise of the will.

I AM all mind, God's Mind. My will is supreme. My will shall cast the decisive vote in the contest between the positive and negative forces within my nature. My will is Spirit active in manifesting the power of my soul.

I have climbed to a height in my evolution where I recognize that I reign supreme. I have dominion over all negative conditions. I have reached the perception of the Absolute Truth.

I will not, for I need not submit to the tyranny of any negative authority. Therefore I will not permit any disease to dominate my flesh or destroy the health and peace of my nature.

I reign supreme in this organization and I exact implicit obedience from every part. I deny and defy all negatives for my knowledge of absolute Truth swallows up every negative assumption.

<blockquote>
Centered in Thee all will be mine
That I have failed to reach.
This gives my soul a perfect joy;
My heart's too full for speech!
</blockquote>

"The I AM is the Way"

From

Christian Larson's

"In Light of the Spirit"

When we consider the many statements that were made by Jesus Christ during his life upon earth, we find that those statements separate themselves into two distinct divisions; and the difference between the two is so marked that we come naturally to the conclusion that they were made in two different states of consciousness. The first division seems to emanate from a consciousness that is almost human, or at any rate, so close to the human that we might say it was human nature in its highest form giving expression to its thought and feeling. The outer division, however, seems to emanate from a consciousness that is so lofty that we conclude that it is the Supreme that is speaking.

The reason why the statements made by Jesus Christ separate themselves into these two divisions is easily explained, because he did possess two distinct forms of consciousness, consciousness of the human and consciousness of the divine. When we consider the human race we find that the majority are conscious only of the human, and therefore give expression only to thoughts that are decidedly human. A few, however, among the more advanced in the human family are developing the consciousness of the divine; and many are learning to understand this consciousness more and more, so that there are moments when we reach such a high and such a fine state of realization that we almost feel as if the wisdom of the Divine were thinking in us or speaking through us. The greater part of the time, however, we are conscious only upon the human plane, and are chiefly concerned with the manifested side of existence.

With Jesus it was different, because he had developed that higher spiritual side of his life, and therefore could live consciously, and in fact absolutely, both in the human and in the divine. He could, when he so desired, come down into the life of the human personality, although his human living was indeed of a very high order. Then, at other times, he could ascend to such heights of spiritual wisdom and power that his words were indeed expressions of the eternal I AM; and one of the most remarkable of those expressions is this, "I AM the Way, the Truth and the Life."

In considering this statement we are referred to a corresponding statement that appears earlier in sacred literature; that is, "Be still and know that I AM God," or paraphrased might read, "Be still and know that the eternal I AM is God"; and indeed the eternal I AM is the Way, the Truth and the Life. We know that it is the eternal I AM that is in reality God, the term "I AM," being but another term for the Divine, the Supreme, the Most High; and therefore we can readily appreciate the great statement, "I AM the Way, the Truth and the Life."

We must remember that the I AM, which indeed is the Way, the Truth and the Life, does not dwell exclusively in any one personality. The I AM may find expression through any personality, and indeed does dwell in the soul of every human being. The eternal I AM is enthroned in the spiritual life of every individual soul; and when we enter into the perfect stillness of the soul the peace that passeth understanding that peace that does pass understanding because in that state there is no understanding large enough or wonderful enough to measure the peace we realize it is in that state of peace which is above reason, which is above ordinary mental activity, which is even above what we usually call thinking, where we may know or discern the presence of the I AM.

When we are in that peace we are in absolute Light, and we do not really think about anything, for the truth is that when we are in the Light we know. It is not necessary to think there in the usual sense of that term, because we know; and here let us remember that there is a marked distinction between thinking and knowing, and between understanding and realization. The process of thinking is a process through which we create thoughts about something that we are trying to understand; but when we know, then we do not have to try to understand or create temporary thoughts about what we are seeking to know. When we know, then the mind is in a state of illumination, and dwells serenely in the perfect realization of the Great Spiritual Light.

We understand therefore that when we are in the peace that passeth understanding, we are above actual mental activities; we are in a state where all these things are felt and realized as absolute states of being; and it is in that realization that we become conscious of the presence and the power of the Eternal I AM.

If we should try to define the I AM to objective intellect, we might liken the I AM to a great White Light enthroned in the soul, and giving expression to its wisdom and power through those higher states of consciousness into which we enter when we are in the glory and light of the soul world. We realize therefore that when we ascend in our consciousness, higher and higher into our own spiritual being, we draw nearer and nearer to the Great White Light that exists upon the spiritual heights of that realm in which the soul forever dwells serene.

When we enter into this lofty state, we meet a wonderful experience; and it is this, that as we become conscious of the life and the presence of the Great White Light, we enter in a measure into that Light, and we feel that we are so perfectly in that Light that we partake of the consciousness of the Eternal I AM. In brief, we feel as if we have become one with the I AM, and can actually make the same great statement, "I AM the Way, the Truth and the Life." In a measure this is true, because we all are one with the I AM in spirit; and when we become conscious of that sublime unity, we partake of the same wisdom and the same power, and also become channels, so to speak, through which the Most High may speak the Word of Eternal Truth.

The statement that "My Father and I are one," illustrates this same experience, because every human entity, spiritually speaking, is one with the Supreme; and when this oneness becomes a reality in consciousness, the Infinite does speak through us, or we give expression to what is in reality the Word of God.

The eternal I AM is individualized in every soul, and therefore we can say that the I AM in ourselves, that is, the Great White Light of the soul, does constitute the Gates Ajar, in our own spiritual being, to the Way, the Truth and the Life. What is more, we find that it is the consciousness of the I AM in our own spiritual existence that constitutes the only secret path to that lofty state wherein we find the Way, the Truth and the Life. We cannot find the Way, the Truth and the Life through any external source not even through the personality of Jesus, or through the personality of any extraordinary soul that might have appeared, or that may appear upon earth.

The secret path to the Way is found only in our own interior consciousness of the I AM individualized in us, or our own spiritual consciousness of the Great White Light enthroned in the secret realms of our own soul. If we would find the Way, we must become conscious of the I AM in ourselves; and it matters not how we may proceed, what system of thought or religion we may follow; those things are of secondary importance. The one thing of supreme importance is that we have this great object in view in every effort, or study of life to become conscious more and more of the I AM the Supreme Spiritual Light reigning supremely within our own spiritual kingdom.

When our attention is concentrated entirely upon that goal, it does not matter what we may call ourselves or what systems of thought we may follow. If we all have that goal, we all are moving in the same direction; and we all are realizing an ever-increasing measure of that Great Light into which we someday shall enter perfectly, and there meet, face to face, the I AM the Infinite the Most High. It is the truth that so long as we all have that lofty goal in view, our minor differences are of no importance whatever; and therefore we should lay them all aside, and try to serve each other more perfectly, so that we may rise in the scale of consciousness to a far greater degree than ever before.

Thus we shall gain more and more of that wisdom and realization that constitutes the key to the mansions of Freedom, of Truth and of Light. Where the human race has erred in the past is in this, that we have sought the Way, the Truth and the Life through the existence of some personality instead of seeking it through the consciousness of the I AM in our own spiritual kingdom; and the race has also mistaken in trying to gain spiritual power through various external methods, or by means that are not identified with the consciousness of the Great White Light within our own spiritual existence; that is, we have gone out on bypaths, so to speak, and have sought wisdom and power through various external sources, thinking that we might climb up some other way. But there is only one way; and the I AM is the Way the consciousness of the I AM enthroned in our own spiritual kingdom.

The more spiritual we become the more perfectly we realize that those who try to seek spiritual power or wisdom through any other source than through the consciousness of the I AM, are trying to climb up some other way; and Jesus did make some very strong statements in that regard, emphasizing, in no uncertain terms, the uselessness of such a course. When we study history, especially the spiritual side of history, we discover that those who have tried to seek spiritual power in some other way have invariably come to grief; and they have in all ages been looked upon as the "black sheep" of the fold. It is always true, that whenever we turn away from the one central path and try to gain higher power in some other way, we enter into a state of living that becomes more or less uncanny.

In other words, we become abnormal, both mentally and physically, and the world tends to shrink from us, feeling instinctively that we are on the wrong path, and therefore will have nothing to do with our doctrines or our personalities. The world as a whole may be more or less in the dark, but humanity does instinctively feel whether an individual is on the path to the Pure White Light, or is living on one of the bypaths, which is indeed a violation of spiritual law; and no one can violate spiritual law without surrounding himself with an atmosphere that is repulsive to sensitive human souls.

On the other hand, it does not matter what our religious beliefs may be, if we are sincere in that connection and do proceed with the one lofty purpose in view that is, to find the Spiritual Light within ourselves, seeking that Light neither, through signs and manifestations, nor through the study of the psychical, the occult or the mystical, but proceed directly and sincerely through the highest light of spiritual consciousness that we may have if we proceed in that manner, there is something about us that the world invariably regards with respect. And even though the world may disagree with us in a measure, still there is that feeling on the part of the world that we are sincere, and that we are seeking the highest good.

In brief, the world discerns intuitively that we are on the right path, and that our consciousness of the Light, as far as we have gone, is the consciousness of the Pure White Light. We shall find a marked difference in all our efforts when we make this our supreme purpose; that is, to become more and more conscious of the Eternal I AM enthroned in our own spiritual kingdom; and when we follow Jesus Christ we do so, not in the sense of depending upon his personality, or expecting to gain anything through his personal existence, but we follow him in this sense, that he revealed, in his life and in his wonderful teachings, the secret path to this sublime consciousness within ourselves through which we may find the I AM which indeed is the Way, the Truth and the Life.

We can readily understand that the consciousness of the I AM as outlined above, must necessarily constitute the true way, because when we are looking for the Way, we are looking for that path that leads into higher states of consciousness, into great spiritual wisdom, into the illumined state, and into the conscious possession of that sublime power that will enable us to understand life to make life as rich, as high, as beautiful, as wonderful and as ideal as the true spiritual life can and will be made.

When we become conscious of the I AM we become conscious of the Light of Wisdom and Truth; we become conscious of that Higher Power that exists inherently in every human soul; and we know that whatever we become conscious of, that we will manifest in mind and body. When we ascend into higher realizations of this same consciousness we find that the mind will go higher and higher into the Light, into the Wisdom and into the Power; and thus we find those very things that do indeed constitute the Way the Way to the Christ consciousness, the Christ life and the life of sublime unity with the Most High.

We also realize that this same consciousness of the I AM must indeed be the truth, because the light of the I AM is the Light of the Eternal, and it is the Pure White Light the Light that reveals the absolute Truth, and Truth of the All in All. In like manner, we understand how this same consciousness of the I AM within our own spiritual kingdom must reveal to us the life we seek the life eternal, the glorified life, the spiritualized life, the life more abundant, the life that is, was and ever more shall be. We knew that the nearer we draw in consciousness to this deeper, higher state of spiritual being, the more fully we realize the existence and the expression of the life that is real life; and therefore our growth in that consciousness must necessarily be followed by larger expressions of all that abides within that life.

We all have experienced, while in silent moments, something in this connection that illustrates clearly the idea that we here have in mind. While resting in those silent moments, we have felt something wonderful within ourselves, within the kingdom of the soul, inspiring the mind to take wings so that we have arisen to those sublime states of realization where we have felt the presence of a power and a life that we knew at once to be the life and the power of the spirit. This life and power thrilled every atom of our being, and we felt as if we were surcharged with a living essence that could not be otherwise than immortal and eternal.

It is in that state that we have become conscious of the life more abundant; for in truth, a great influx of higher spiritual life has entered consciousness, mind and personality, sometimes to such a great degree that we were literally overwhelmed with glory and power from On High. It is in this experience that we fully realize the meaning of the great statement, "I came that ye might have life, and that ye might have it more abundantly"; for the truth is, that when the I AM comes into consciousness; or in other words, when we ascend in consciousness so that we meet the presence of the I AM in us, it is then that this wonderful influx of spiritual life appears in our own being.

When we touch the I AM within ourselves, we naturally receive the greater life of the I AM; and we always touch the I AM within when we enter into the spiritual consciousness of the I AM. The same great truth is emphasized by the statement "Follow Me"; because we must follow the Christ or the Christ consciousness if we would enter into this wonderful realm of spiritual illumination. But it is not the personal man, or the personality of Jesus that we are to follow. It is the Great Light that the Christ revealed that we are to follow; and we follow that light when we consecrate thought upon the marvelous spiritual within, and seek the kingdom of God in our own interior life and soul.

The one thing of importance to be considered herewith is this, that we may find the Way, the Truth and the Life only through the inner consciousness of the I AM that sublime expression of the Most High that is enthroned in every soul. The I AM is the Great Eternal Light centralized in the soul and enthroned in the spiritual kingdom of every individual soul. We must look to that light, consecrate attention upon that light, and never try to find the secret path in some other way.

We must enter through the door of the I AM; and we do enter through the door of the I AM when we become conscious more and more of the life, the power and the spirit of the eternal I AM existing within our own spiritual being. Every moment that we might spend in trying to secure these things in some other way is so much time and effort lost. We realize therefore that we all might advance wonderfully, both in mind and spirit, and rise remarkably in the scale of existence, if we would give every attention to this one sublime source. Our purpose in the future must be to consecrate attention upon the real door of the Spirit, the consciousness of the I AM; and seek the Way, the Truth, and the Life through the spirit of the I AM as it Is upon the heights of our own spiritual world; and to this end we must learn to understand the great statement "Be still and know that I AM God," for the Eternal I AM is indeed God.

When objective thought or objective reason is stilled, it is then that the soul may ascend into that calm serene attitude in search of the Light in its purity, in search of the peace that passeth understanding, in search of supernal heights, in search of the Great White Light. And when all these things are found, then the soul does find the Way, the Truth and the Life the soul does meet in reality the radiant countenance of the Christ, the Glorified Presence of the Most High.

"What AM I?"

From Various Chapters of

Orison Swett Marden's

"Prosperity, How To Attract It"

What AM I?

I AM _____?

I AM your best friend in time of need.

I can do for you what those who love you most are powerless to do without my aid.

I AM the oil that smoothes the troubled waters of life. I straighten out difficulties and remove obstacles that will yield to nothing else.

I AM a supporter of faith, a spur to ambition, a tonic to aspiration, an invaluable aid to people who are struggling to make their dreams come true.

I give a man a fine sense of independence, a feeling of security in regard to the future, which increases his strength and ability and enables him to work with more vigor and spontaneity.

I AM a stepping-stone to better things; a hope builder; an enemy of discouragement, because I take away one of the greatest causes of worry, anxiety, and fear.

I increase self-respect and self-confidence, and give a feeling of comfort and assurance that nothing else can give. I impart a consciousness of power that makes multitudes, who otherwise would cringe and crawl, hold up their heads and carry themselves with dignity.

I open the door to many opportunities for self-culture and to social and business advancement. I have enabled tens of thousands of young men, who made sacrifices to get me, to take advantage of splendid opportunities which those who did not have me were obliged to let go by.

I increase your importance in the world and your power to do good.

I make people think well of your ability, increase their confidence in you; give you standing, capital, an assured position, influence, credit, and many of the good things of life that without me would be unattainable.

I AM a shock-absorber for the jolts of life, a buffer between you and the rough knocks of the world. The man or woman who doesn't make an honest, determined effort to get me is lacking in one of the fundamental qualities that make for the happiness, the prosperity and well-being of the whole race.

Millions of mothers and children have suffered all sorts of hardships and humiliations because husbands and fathers lacked this practical quality, which would have saved themselves and those dependent on them so much suffering and misery.

Multitudes have spent their declining years in homeless wretchedness, or eked out a miserable existence in humiliating dependence on the grudging charity of relatives, while other multitudes have died in the poorhouse, because they failed to make friends with me in their youth.

I AM one of the most reliable aids in the battle of life, the struggle for independence; ever ready to help you in an emergency . . sickness in your family, accident or loss, a crisis in your business . . whatever it may be. You can always rely on me to step into the breach and do my work quietly, effectively, without bluster.

I AM . . . A LITTLE READY CASH

What AM I?

I AM _____ ?

I AM the great paralyzer of ability, the murderer of aspiration and ambition, the destroyer of energy, the killer of opportunity.

I AM the cause of more suffering, more human misery and loss, more tragedies and wretchedness than any other one thing.

I have cursed more human beings, arrested the development of more fine ability, strangled more genius and stifled more talent than anything else in the world.

I have shortened vast multitudes of lives and sent more people to the insane asylum, to crime and suicide than men dream of.

I cause chemical changes in the brain which cripple efficiency and ruin careers.

I deprive human beings of more things that are good for them, things that fit their nature, and that they were intended to enjoy, than any other one agent.

I cause men and women to wear poor, shabby clothes, to look dejected and forlorn, when it is the right of every human being to look up, to be well dressed, attractive, and happy.

I shut out the sun of hope and cause men to see everything in a distorted light because I make them look on the shadow side of things.

I devitalize people and make chronic invalids of men and women who should be enjoying perfect health.

I AM the devil's most effective instrument. If he can once get the bare suggestion of me into the human consciousness at the psychological moment, he can work destruction to the most ambitious, the greatest genius.

I starve and stunt minds, and keep vast multitudes of people in ignorance.

I usually attack a man when he is down, when things have gone wrong, and he is feeling blue. When he is tired, fatigued, devitalized, I find an easy entrance to his mind, because then his courage is not so keen, his brain is not so alert, and he has less dare in his nature.

I find that the best time to work on my victims is in the afternoon. In the morning men are too vigorous mentally, have too much vitality and energy, too much courage, to give in to me, but along in the afternoon when the body and brain begin to weary of work, and the whole man feels a bit fagged, I can tackle the great mental scheme which was in the forefront of the brain in the forenoon, when the faculties were clean-cut, and unless my victim is alert I soon have him under my control.

I AM the greatest human deceiver. Once I get into the mind, I can make a giant believe he is a pygmy, and of no account. I can cut down his self respect until in his own estimation he is a very ordinary man.

I have a twin brother, Doubt, who is called the great traitor. He is always ready to help me to finish my little game. We work together, and when under our control it is impossible for a man to be resourceful, original, or effective.

I creep into a man's mind after he has resolved to branch out on new lines, to step out from the beaten path and blaze his own way, and weaken his ardor, dampen his enthusiasm, and make him feel inefficient and helpless.

I whisper in his ear, "Go slow; better be careful. Many abler men than you have fallen down trying to do that very thing. It is not the time to start this thing; you had better wait, wait, wait."

I haven't a single redeeming thing in my nature, and yet I have more influence with the human race than has any one of the finer, nobler qualities which help to bring man up to the height of his possibilities.

I AM . . . DISCOURAGEMENT

What AM I?

I AM _____ ?

I AM the vital principle of life . . the greatest of all success and happiness assets.

I AM that which gives the plus quality to human beings. I put pep, ginger, vim, into human effort.

I AM the source of physical and mental power. I give the body vigor and buoyancy, the brain vital energy and originality.

I AM your best friend . . the friend of the high and lowly, the rich and the poor alike . . but, be he king or beggar, who violates my laws must pay the penalty.

I AM often sought in vain by the man who rides in his limousine, but am generally found in the company of the man who walks to his work and takes plenty of exercise.

I AM the great multiplier of ability, the buttress of initiative, of courage, of self-confidence, the backbone of enthusiasm, without which nothing worthwhile was ever accomplished.

I AM the greatest constructive power in the life of man. Without me his faith weakens, his ambition sags, his ardor oozes out, his courage faints, his self-confidence departs, his accomplishment is nil.

Without me wealth is a mockery, a palatial home a bitter disappointment.

Next to life itself, I AM the greatest gift God has given to man; the millionaire who has lost me in piling up his fortune would give all his millions to get me back again. I AM that which gives buoyancy to life, which makes you magnetic, joyous; forceful, which brings out your resourcefulness and inventiveness, that which raises efficiency to its maximum and enables you to make the most of your ability.

I increase every one of your forty or fifty mental faculties a hundredfold.

I AM the leader of them all. When I AM present they are up, at their best; when I AM absent, they are down, at their worst.

I AM the friend of progress, the stimulator of ambition, the encourager of effort, the great essential to efficiency, to success, the promoter of long life and happiness.

I AM a joy bringer. Where I go, good cheer goes. Where I AM not, depression, discouragement, the "blues," are present. My absence means declining powers, often thwarted ambition, blighted hopes, mediocrity, failure, a shortened life.

The wise man guards me as the apple of his eye; the fool often abuses and loses me through ignorance, indifference or neglect.

I AM . . . GOOD HEALTH

What AM I?

I AM _____ ?

I AM that which is back of all achievement, which has led the way to success, to happiness, through the ages.

I crossed an unknown ocean with Columbus, who without me would never have discovered America.

I was with Washington at Valley Forge; and but for me he would not have succeeded in liberating the American colonies and making them a nation.

I went through the Civil War with Lincoln, and guided his pen when he wrote the Emancipation Proclamation that freed millions of human beings from slavery.

I was with the English patriots who forced King John to sign that great charter of human rights . . the Magna Charta.

I was back of those who forced the French Revolution . . and of those who signed the American Declaration of Independence.

I was with Christ when all his disciples and friends had fled; and I cheered and comforted the martyrs at the stake . . all the men and women who gave their lives to maintain the truths he taught.

I crossed the ocean with Cyrus W. Field fifty times before his great undertaking, the ocean cable, was perfected. I was on the ship with him when the cable parted in mid-ocean, after the first message had passed over it, and gave him courage to persist when the work had to be done all over again.

I AM the locksmith who can unlock all doors, whom no obstacle can hold back, no difficulty or disaster dishearten, no misfortune swerve from my purpose.

I AM a friend to the down-and-outs, the unfortunates, those to whom life has been a great disappointment. If these people would take hold of me I would turn them around so that they would face their goal and go toward it instead of turning their back on it and going in the opposite direction; they would face the sun and let the shadows fall behind instead of in front of them as in the past.

I AM a booster, an optimist, one who always sees something of hope in every human being, for I know that there is a God in every one; that men and women are gods in the making; that they are all capable of doing infinitely more, infinitely better things, than they have yet done.

No matter how bad the conditions which confront me, I wear a smile, for I know that the sun is always behind the clouds and that after a time the storm will pass and the sun will shine again.

I see triumph beyond temporary defeat. I look past obstacles which discourage most people, for I know that they become smaller as one approaches them; and experience has shown me that but a very small fraction of the things which people dread, fear, and worry about ever happen.

If you know me, if you believe in me, work with me, cling to me, no matter how full of failures and disappointments your past has been, I will help you to overcome adverse conditions and crown you with success, for I conquer all difficulties.

I AM . . . FAITH

What AM I?

I AM _____?

I AM stored-up happiness.

I lead the way to peace, power, and plenty. I bring you freedom from anxiety and worry over the living problem.

I AM a friend alike of the rich and the poor.

I AM common sense applied to life in all sorts of ways.

I AM a tower of strength in youth and a staff in old age.

I increase hope, confidence, assurance, certainty as to the future.

I was one of the chief factors in the winning of the World War.

I AM the best form of insurance against poverty and failure. I remove the shadow of the poorhouse.

I make for health, for efficiency, for the highest possible welfare of the individual.

I kill that "rainy day" dread; in fact, I do away with the "rainy day" altogether.

I put hope into the heart of man, a light into human eyes that was never there before.

I put people in a position to take advantage of all sorts of opportunities for investment, for advancement, to take advantage of chances that, but for me, would be lost.

I mean the best physicians, the most skilled surgeons, the best hospitals in case of need, as well as the best health resorts.

I make possible a needed vacation, rest, recreation and travel. I mean leisure, more living with natural art and with the beautiful things in the world.

I mean better opportunities for your children, better schools, better clothing, a more refining environment, greater security for their future.

I show you how to make the most of your income; how to expend the margin to the best advantage; how to make the wisest investments of your time, your strength and your ability as well as your money.

I AM the friend of man, a civilization builder. I not only give an upward tendency to the life of the individual, but also to the life of a nation.

I sustain and preserve the highest welfare of the race.

I safeguard the future; I enable you to work with confidence, to look up and not down, to rise superior to your surroundings.

I keep thousands of people out of the penitentiary; prevent them from committing theft and other crimes.

I increase the confidence of others in struggling young men and add tremendously to their credit.

I AM an employee's best recommendation, for I belong to a large and most excellent family. Every employer knows that the employee who cultivates me has many other sterling qualities, such as honesty, thoroughness, ambition, reliability, foresight, prudence. I AM a symbol of character, of stability, of self-control; a proof that a man is not a victim of his appetites and weaknesses, but their master.

I AM often the savoir of a man, cutting off indulgences and vicious habits, putting health in the place of dissipation and insuring a clear brain instead of a cloudy, befuddled one.

I AM the enemy of that great curse of mankind . . debt . . which wrecks multitudes of homes, causes divorce, blasts love, and destroys all peace of mind.

I AM that which helps a man to lift his head above the crowd; to be independent, self-reliant, and to stand for something in the world.

Multitudes of families are homeless, moneyless, and are enduring all sorts of hardship, privation, and humiliation because the husbands and fathers never took me into partnership.

The failure army, today, is largely recruited by people who never learned to know me, who ridiculed the suggestion of needing me, who rather despised and looked down on me as standing for meanness and penuriousness and as being an enemy of their enjoyment.

I AM the best friend of woman. I make her a better businesswoman, a better housekeeper, a better wife and mother, a better citizen. I help her to make herself independent, self-reliant, and teach her how to finance herself.

However you make your living, whether by the work of your hand or of your brain, in a trade or in a profession, at home or in the shop, whether your income be small or large, you will always be placed at a disadvantage, will always be taking chances with your future security and happiness, unless you have me as a working partner.

I AM an incentive to high living, the simple life and high thinking. I urge spending upward, living upward, dwelling in honesty, in simplicity, living the life that is worthwhile, the genuine life, the life that will give enduring satisfaction.

I AM the beginning of real success; that which puts a foundation under your air castles, that which makes your dreams come true, which builds that "home of my own" to which every healthy, ambitious young person looks forward as the culmination of his hopes.

I AM . . . THRIFT

I AM Notes:

I AM Notes:

I AM Notes:

The Power of I AM 3 - David Allen

I AM Notes:

The Power of I AM 3 - David Allen

I AM Notes:

Metaphysical / Law of Attraction Books

David Allen - The Power of I AM (2014), The Power of I AM - Volume 2 (2015), The Power of I AM - Volume 3 (2017)

David Allen - The Creative Power of Thought, Man's Greatest Discovery (2017)

David Allen - The Secrets, Mysteries & Powers of The Subconscious Mind (2017)

David Allen - The Money Bible - The Secrets of Attracting Prosperity (2017)

David Allen - Your Faith Is Your Fortune, Your Unlimited Power

The Neville Goddard Collection (All 10 of his books plus 2 Lecture series) (2016)

Neville Goddard - Assumptions Harden Into Facts: The Book (2016)

Neville Goddard - Imagination: The Redemptive Power in Man (2016)

Neville Goddard - The World is At Your Command - The Very Best of Neville Goddard (2017)

Neville Goddard - Imagining Creates Reality - 365 Mystical Daily Quotes (2017)

Neville Goddard's Interpretation of Scripture (2018)

The Definitive Christian D. Larson Collection (6 Volumes, 30 books) (2014)

www.ingramcontent.com/pod-product-compliance
Lightning Source LLC
Chambersburg PA
CBHW021124300426
44113CB00006B/277